*For Delaine,
whose inspiring speeches brought this
series into being— best wishes,
Doris and María 12/12/95*

AMERICAN WOMEN SPEAK

Voices of American Women in Public Life

Women Speak Series No. 2

Introduction by Ruth Mandel

Doris Earnshaw and María Elena Raymond, Editors

Alta Vista Press, P.O. Box 73675, Davis, CA 95617
1995

Published by

Alta Vista Press, P.O. Box 73675, Davis, CA 95617
Women Speak Series No. 2

Photographs of Hilda Solis, Doris Earnshaw and María Elena Raymond
by Sirlin Photographers, Sacramento, California
Photograph of Christine Todd Whitman by Linz Photography,
Toms River, New Jersey

Cover design by Jeanne Pietrzak, Graphic Gold, Davis, CA

The speeches in the book are published by permission.

Library of Congress Catalog Card Number
95-80502

ISBN: 0-9640574-2-5

©Doris Earnshaw and María Elena Raymond

Introduction ©1995 by Dr. Ruth Mandel

ALL RIGHTS RESERVED

PRINTED IN THE UNITED STATES OF AMERICA

NOVEMBER 1995

FIRST EDITION

10 9 8 7 6 5 4 3 2 1

Table of Contents

                                                                                                            Page

FOREWORD   Doris Earnshaw and María Elena Raymond vii

INTRODUCTION Ruth Mandel, Director, Eagleton Institute of Politics, Rutgers University ix

HILLARY RODHAM CLINTON, First Lady of the United States of America 3
    "It is time for us to say... and for the world to hear, that it is no longer acceptable to discuss women's rights as separate from human rights."

TIPPER GORE, Mental Health Advisor to the President 15
    "Government must think of children in every policy decision we make."

NANCY LANDON KASSEBAUM, U.S. Senator, Kansas 23
    "If we did not now have the United Nations, we would be forced to invent it. But if we could invent the U.N., we would not invent the one we now have."

DIANNE FEINSTEIN, U.S. Senator, California 33
    "I am quite familiar with firearms... I found my assassinated colleague and put a finger through a bullet hole trying to get (a pulse)..."

KAY BAILEY HUTCHISON, U.S. Senator, Texas 41
    "Economic strength is just as important as military might."

CHRISTINE TODD WHITMAN, Governor, New Jersey 47
    "...we will get better results by putting people and neighborhoods at the heart of everything we do."

ANN RICHARDS, Governor, Texas (1990-1994) 53
    "...it is not so much a matter of choosing your final destination as it is deciding you will travel your own course..."

PATRICIA SCHROEDER, U.S. Representative, Colorado 61
    "Playing on women's ambivalence about who we are and what we want is big business in America."

CORRINE BROWN, U.S. Representative, Florida 67
    "The shape of a district is not mentioned in the Constitution but representation is — it's guaranteed."

— Contents —

	page
TILLIE K. FOWLER, U.S. Representative, Florida	73

"*Current defense policy is a runaway train headed for disaster...*"

CYNTHIA McKINNEY, U.S. Representative, Georgia 77
  "*...American arms should not be sold and U.S. military training should not be provided to governments that oppose American principles.*"

ELIZABETH DOLE, President, American Red Cross 83
  "*...our greatest obstacle — that we are women in a world of men — is really an enormous opportunity, if we will just see it that way.*"

LYNN MARTIN, U.S. Secretary of Labor (1991-1993) 91
  "*I found out that I wanted to run for president...*"

MADELEINE MAY KUNIN, U.S. Deputy Secretary of Education 97
  "*We have moved from the politics of blame... to the politics of results...*"

JEANE J. KIRKPATRICK, U.S. Ambassador to the United Nations (1981-1985) .. 107
  "*...governments with the worst human rights records are also the most likely to commit aggression against neighbors, to start wars, and to impose their preferred positions on others by force.*"

HILDA L. SOLIS, State Senator, California 117
  "*Domestic violence is a poison not just within a household, but outside that home, affecting all our lives.*"

DEBORAH J. GLICK, State Assemblymember, New York 121
  "*And I have heard people say that to be lesbian or gay is unnatural; it is only unnatural if you are not lesbian or gay. It is very natural to me.*"

ROSALIE E. WAHL, Justice, Supreme Court, Minnesota (1977-1994) 125
  "*...we had better look to the way people of color perceive they are treated by our courts, and how they are treated, to preserve the integrity of our system of justice...*"

CHERYL A. LAU, General Counsel, U.S. House of Representatives 135
  "*One of the most important four-letter words is never used by graffiti artists... That word is VOTE.*"

INDEX OF ISSUES 139

Foreword

The explosion of material about contemporary women leaders contains few collections of their own words. We can buy posters, sociological studies and even "Great Women Paper Dolls." Yet a respected journal such as *Vital Speeches* has a ratio of one woman speaker to 10 men, and many issues include no women. So, while biographies and studies proliferate, the voices of women in public life are less available than their importance deserves. We have sought to correct that imbalance, and hope others will share our fascination with the close-up picture of women at work in public life that this book provides.

As we began our search for innovative speeches, we discovered the influence of television on speech writing. Television, with its demand for six-second sound bites and rapid-fire answers to prearranged questions, makes talk more important than thought. This oral style invites repetition of an opinion, not the logical development of an argument. Narrow focus wins the day, not background information, technical detail or leisured and rhetorical flourish. Indeed, some office staff members reacted with astonishment to our request for printed speeches. Others responded that their chief used only notes or talking points, and could not provide texts, or if they had texts, that their chief changed every text depending on the moment and the audience.

Several instances of impromptu speech are here: Dianne Feinstein's famous reply when a Senate colleague referred to her as "a gentle lady unfamiliar with firearms" and New York Assemblymember Deborah Glick's hasty reduction of a prepared 15-minute speech to a two-minute statement. Elizabeth Dole tells a story about getting out of a tight spot in her first court appearance as a lawyer by suggesting that a lion from the zoo should be called as a witness.

Other women are famous for their ad lib humor. Tales of Ann Richard's wit continue to circulate. We like the one about her response to a California legislator, at a Beverly Hills Hotel conference, who poked his head in the room where Texas Governor Richards was chairing a women's committee meeting. To his question, "What are you girls doing?" she smiled and said in her Texas drawl, "We're planning a picnic. Sally here is bringing the potato salad and Jane will serve the coffee — and what are you doing?"

Women have always lived in the oral speech world. They continue to be storytellers in forums from children's bedsides to elegant salons. Their gossip has been an informal social control for people shut out of formal avenues of power. But now and in the future, as women enter the formal patterns of power, their hopes and ideas will increasingly be encoded in written form. From those centuries of formal silence, women inherit the keen sight of the silent observer. "...My body is an endless eye, through which, unfortunately, I see everything," writes the poet Gloria Fuertes.

One of the results of that silent position that women occupied is the development of intuition, which Peter Abelard called the most certain knowledge. It is the subject of Elizabeth Dole's astute analysis. With her amusing phrase, "Why can't a woman be more like a woman?" she shows a confidence in and respect for women's rationality and instinct, the ability to make a rapid estimation of the whole scene. The power of that rationality can change the world. It might be called common sense. For example, Rosa Parks' plain "I'm tired of Jim Crow" brought a new consciousness to American race relations. As we read the many submissions for this book, we looked for depth of conviction that stems from that innate, intuitive rationality.

With refreshing candor, Lynn Martin gives a startling vision of a woman contemplating a run for the presidency. We note U.S. Senator Feinstein's reliance on detail in her passionate appeal for gun control. Congresswoman Corrine Brown's talk on affirmative action comes out of the long troubled history of race in America, while retired Minnesota Supreme Court Justice Rosalie Wahl's challenge to the legal system is framed by her years in the courtroom.

Civil society occupies the expertise of U.S. Senator Kay Bailey Hutchison, New Jersey Governor Christine Todd Whitman and California Senator Hilda L. Solis. Legislators and administrators, they speak about the relationship of government to our economic and private lives. In the contemporary world, their vision rightly makes government equally involved in trade, urban affairs and domestic safety.

The world beyond our borders attracts the attention of at least four speakers. Hillary Clinton's "magic" presence in international gatherings, as Madeleine Albright has called it, shows in her affectionate remembrance of Eleanor Roosevelt and in her powerful denunciation of worldwide abuses that target women. Former U.N. Ambassador Jeane Kirkpatrick connects China's abuse of internal dissidents with the approach it may take in future international relations. Senator Nancy Landon Kassebaum's seldom acknowledged but crucial efforts to overturn apartheid in South Africa validate her strong words to African ambassadors. Governor Richards speaks warmly in Spanish to a gathering of prominent Mexicans and Texans.

We sought to make this book inclusive and nonpartisan. Not surprisingly, we found that certain issues inspire women across party lines to put people first. In American life, women leaders voice a determination to do better by children and working mothers. Tipper Gore forcefully points out our need to face the awful statistics on the plight of many children. Congresswoman Patricia Schroeder calls for the "family-friendly" workplace. Governor Whitman puts neighborhoods at the heart of her urban policy.

In foreign relations, Congresswoman Tillie Fowler urges us to face the dark potential of defeat if we reduce our war capability too far. Congresswoman Cynthia McKinney asks that we work to lessen the damage the world arms trade causes, and to take responsibility for not arming dictatorships. Jeane Kirkpatrick's analysis of the link between totalitarian attitudes and violence goes to the heart of all the concerns these speeches express. We believe that as women enter legislatures around the world in significant numbers, they will use their power of realism to probe abuses of human rights formerly considered acceptable.

We begin by excerpting a poem we discovered in a book from the early 1930s when the women's vote was new. We close with Cheryl Lau's exposé of behind-the-scenes work to keep the vote a vital part of everyone's participation in public life.

We wish to thank the many women who submitted material for this project and the hard-working staff members who assisted in a thousand details. Robin Miller of the Department of State's Protocol Office advised us on name placement. Mary Doty and Rebecca LaVally worked as an outstanding team on computer printing and copy editing. Jeanne Pietrzak of Graphic Gold advised us at every stage. We thank Kate Karpilow, who put us in touch with Ruth Mandel, and Dr. Mandel for her enthusiasm and support. We are grateful to Evelyne Rominger, Richard Raymond, Ann Evans, David Thompson, and the faculty and staff in Comparative Literature at the University of California, Davis.

The Editors

Introduction

Public speaking has a long and honored history. In the Western world, the tradition of oratory and public rhetoric, especially when eloquent, has been respected since at least the ancient Greeks. It is a tradition associated with men's public voices, the familiar names stretching across time and place from Demosthenes and Cicero to Thomas Jefferson, Frederick Douglass, Abraham Lincoln, Franklin Delano Roosevelt, and Martin Luther King Jr.

The examples of public outspokenness by women reflected in this volume emerge after a long history of public silence and from a deeply rooted tradition of disapproval of women taking active public roles. For centuries, women, like children, were expected to be seen, not heard; silence was the preferred "sound" for women outside the kitchen and nursery. The space of public sound had been reserved for men, and women who presumed to enter it were condemned. Men uttered the pronouncements, judgments and verdicts, policies, blessings and sermons, and men passed along the culture's received wisdom. Even in Shakespeare's England, ruled by a female monarch, men were enlisted to play female parts on stage.

Although in the earliest days they broke the sound barrier at great risk, American women have been going public for some time. Historically, uppity women were punished with everything from mild disapproval and ridicule to indictment for witchcraft. There were always exceptions and varieties of tolerance: most notably, the Quakers offered a well-known early supportive environment for everyone — women as well as men — to speak up in church and share their religious experiences. By the second half of the 19th century, an Elizabeth Cady Stanton could spend many months each year traveling from town to town on the Lyceum circuit to address audiences about women's rights and the campaign for suffrage. Other outspoken women had begun appearing on public platforms in noteworthy, if small, numbers earlier in the 19th century. Moved by religious belief, conscience, moral outrage, personal encounters with injustice, and activist family members and acquaintances, women emerged as advocates for various causes. The early women's public voices most familiar to us from that period — among them Angelina and Sara Grimké, Fanny Wright, Susan B. Anthony, Sojourner Truth, Elizabeth Cady Stanton, Frances Willard — spoke out against slavery, for female suffrage, temperance and other issues of their day.

Between then and the 1960s, the voices of woman activists were joined by those singular individuals whose talents and good fortune made it possible for them to leap over conventional barriers. Exceptional women like Emma Goldman, Elizabeth Gurley Flynn, Margaret Sanger, Ida B. Wells, Eleanor Roosevelt, Mary McLeod Bethune, Margaret Chase Smith and others both equally well-known and less widely recognized in politics and other arenas managed to project their voices beyond the confines of their families and speak to larger audiences, from their neighborhoods to the nation.

Twentieth-century American women have stepped forward as leaders and public reformers in many efforts to bring about change, especially progressive change — for workers' rights and organized labor, for legalizing birth control information, for anti-lynching laws, for women's rights, free speech, child labor laws, and later for civil rights, nuclear test bans, peace, welfare rights, abortion rights, gay and lesbian rights, Native American rights, consumer rights, laws against drunk driving, and more. Far from monolithic in their beliefs, women have been active in support of issues and movements across the ideological spectrum.

Today women's public voices are more common, whether in guiding negotiations and deliberations, or speaking over airwaves and microphones, in courtrooms and boardrooms, from pulpits as well as political platforms.

American Women Speak: Voices of American Women in Public Life collects examples of the spoken word from those whose voices emanate from the political arena, largely from women who have served in a variety of public offices and positions inside the United States electoral system during the 1990s. Just 25 years ago a collection of examples from this many political women would virtually have exhausted the range of possibilities. Eight women who appear in this volume either serve or have served in the United States Senate or House; they were selected from 55 who serve in Congress today and a few dozen former members. Twenty-five years ago, there would have been but 11 women sitting in the House and Senate and a handful of former members from whom to choose. In these pages there are also current and former governors, state legislators, a lieutenant governor, a judge, a former ambassador to the United Nations, appointed officials, and the women who serve the public as first lady and as wife of the vice president.

Even with so many more women with high political platforms to choose among today, women still constitute a mere 10 percent of all members of the House and Senate, and Governor Christine Todd Whitman of New Jersey, represented in this volume, is the sole woman to serve as a state's chief executive in 1995. While today we hear many more women than ever before speaking up in politics, anything like a true balance of women's and men's voices in the leadership of our public world is still a distant dream.

The women in this volume are outstanding for their individual achievements, and they symbolize significant progress for American women in general. They come from both major political parties and a variety of political roles. Yet it must be noted that this small group of leaders cannot be representative of the richly varied female population in the United States, or even the full range of American political women. This collection of their public comments provides but a hint of the complex ideological and political variations, the differences in viewpoints and experiences among women in various areas of today's national political life. These women are active and successful in mainstream electoral politics in one way or another; other women can be found in other political arenas — for example, in advocacy, issue and protest politics, in social reform and in many areas of grassroots activism.

It must also be noted that this set of speeches makes no pretense of reflecting the sum and substance of these women's political thinking or the capacity of women for impressive oratory. Some are simply direct statements about immediate issues; others offer more thoughtful reflections. Some are not even standard speeches, but rather texts of women addressing themselves in public to a variety of issues and talking about them in various spoken formats — at symposia, at organization meetings and conventions, or in bill introductions and on the legislative floor, in testimony, hearings, question-and-answer sessions or press conferences.

Altogether they do represent an important sound in American life — the sound of political women talking, the sound of sopranos and altos in places hitherto reserved for tenors and baritones. This is the sound of women addressing a variety of public situations and issues and not limited to speaking solely from and about the confines of private or domestic life. These talks illustrate the range of issues which women leaders tackle — including the importance of voting and voting rights, affirmative action, women's rights and human rights, assault weapons and violence, The North Atlantic Treaty Organization, the defense budget, the sale of arms, The North American Free Trade Agreement, foreign affairs, health care, domestic violence, running for the presidency, and much more.

The editors of *American Women Speak* correctly believe that the majority gender must be heard from, and that what women have to say should be widely available. This book takes a worthwhile first step by identifying, collecting and sharing the public utterances of contemporary women who have chosen the political arena for making their contributions to the greater society. Deserving of our attention and respect, they are distinguished pioneers in a generation of women who have dared to speak out, and, in so doing, have overcome their individual and their collective gender history. As Madeleine May Kunin says here about our system of education, "Girls sometimes are rewarded for being quiet and sitting with their hands folded in their laps. Boys are rewarded for waving their arms."

As a society, we must yet learn how to listen and really hear the varied voices of American women. Notwithstanding over a quarter of a century of enormous change in women's lives and in the life of the nation, we are largely tone deaf when it comes to hearing women, much less paying them heed. One would hope also that women, having for so long been discouraged, even prevented, from having a public voice, would accept it as their special responsibility to be particularly sensitive to the concerns of others who are not heard. Hillary Rodham Clinton says in these pages of Eleanor Roosevelt, "Anyone who did not have a voice was someone for whom she spoke." That would surely be a proper and noble use for the voices of women with new powers of public speech.

Ruth B. Mandel
Eagleton Institute of Politics
Rutgers University
New Brunswick, New Jersey

American Women Speak

My Vote

If by my vote I help to bring
 a time when war's no more,
And men are brothers of one blood
 the whole world o'er...

Then I have done my very best
 To help a world in pain;
So take my vote and count it:
 I have not lived in vain.

Dora Ward

Contemporary American Women Poets
Tooni Gordi, editor
Henry Harrison, 430 Sixth Avenue, New York, 1936

Hillary Rodham Clinton

Hillary Rodham Clinton served as first lady of Arkansas for 12 years, from 1978 to 1980 and 1982 through 1992. In addition to fulfilling her duties as the state's first lady, she worked as a full-time partner in a law firm and chaired the Arkansas Education Standards Committee. Clinton founded the Arkansas Advocates for Children and Families. She introduced a pioneering program called Arkansas' Home Instruction Program for Preschool Youth, which trains parents to work with their children in preschool preparedness and literacy. Clinton also served on the board of directors of the Arkansas Children's Hospital. In recognition of her professional and personal accomplishments, she was named Arkansas Woman of the Year in 1983 and Arkansas Mother of the Year in 1984.

Hillary Diane Rodham was born in Chicago, Illinois, on October 26, 1947. She grew up with her two brothers in Park Ridge, Illinois. Clinton entered Wellesley College in 1965. Graduating with high honors, she enrolled in Yale Law School, where she served on the board of editors of the *Yale Review of Law and Social Action*. In 1973, Clinton became a staff attorney for the Children's Defense Fund. A year later she joined the Impeachment Inquiry staff of the Judiciary Committee of the U.S. House of Representatives to work on the Watergate impeachment proceedings.

She married Bill Clinton in 1975. The couple taught on the law faculty of the University of Arkansas at Fayetteville. Their daughter, Chelsea, was born in 1980.

When Bill Clinton took office as president of the United States in 1993, he appointed the first lady to head his Task Force on National Health Care Reform. She brings to her role as first lady of the United States her own special talents, experience, style and interests. On many occasions, Hillary Clinton has spoken about the need "to find the right balance in our lives." For her, the elements of that balance are family, work and public service.

Hillary Rodham Clinton

First Lady of the United States

Hillary Rodham Clinton

[Remarks delivered to the United Nations Fourth World Conference on Women, Beijing, China, September 5, 1995.]

Thank you very much, Madame Gertrude Mongella, for your dedicated work that has brought us to this point.

Distinguished delegates and guests, I would like to thank the secretary general of the United Nations for inviting me to be part of this important United Nations Fourth World Conference on Women. This is truly a celebration — a celebration of the contributions women make in every aspect of life: in the home, on the job, in the community, as mothers, wives, sisters, daughters, learners, workers, citizens and leaders.

It is also a coming together, much the way women come together every day in every country. We come together in fields and in factories. In village markets and supermarkets. In living rooms and board rooms. Whether it is while playing with our children in the park, or washing clothes in a river, or taking a break at the office water cooler, we come together and talk about our aspirations and concerns. And time and again, our talk turns to our children and our families.

However different we may appear, there is far more that unites us than divides us. We share a common future. And we are here to find common ground so that we may help bring new dignity and respect to women and girls all over the world — and in so doing, bring new strength and stability to families as well.

By gathering in Beijing, we are focusing world attention on issues that matter most in the lives of women and their families: access to education, health care, jobs, and credit, the chance to enjoy basic legal and human rights and to participate fully in the political life of their countries.

There are some who question the reason for this conference. Let them listen to the voices of women in their homes, neighborhoods, and workplaces. There are some who wonder whether the lives of women and girls matter to economic and political progress around the globe. Let them look at the women gathered here and at Huairou [nearby site of concurrent conference of non-governmental organizations]: the homemakers, nurses, teachers, lawyers, policymakers, and women who run their own businesses.

It is conferences like this that compel governments and peoples everywhere to listen, look and face the world's most pressing problems. Wasn't it after the women's conference in Nairobi 10 years ago that the world focused for the first time on the crisis of domestic violence? Earlier today, I participated in a World Health Organization forum. In that forum we talked about ways that government officials, non-governmental organizations, and individual citizens are working to address the health problems of women and girls. Tomorrow, I will attend a gathering of the United Nations Development Fund for Women. There, the discussion will focus on local — and highly successful — programs that give hard-working women access to credit so they can improve their own lives and the lives of their families.

What we are learning around the world is if women are healthy and educated, their families will flourish. If women are free from violence, their families will flourish. If women have a chance to work and earn as full and equal partners in society, their families will flourish. And when families flourish, communities and nations will flourish. That is why every woman, every man, every child, every family, and every nation on our planet does have a stake in the discussion that takes place here.

Over the past 25 years, I have worked persistently on issues relating to women, children and families. Over the past two and a half years, I have had the opportunity to learn more about the challenges facing women in my own country and around the world.

I have met new mothers in Indonesia who come together regularly in their village to discuss nutrition, family planning, and baby care. I have met working parents in Denmark who talk about the comfort they feel in knowing that their children can be cared for in creative, safe, and nurturing after-school centers. I have met women in South Africa who helped lead the struggle to end apartheid and are now helping build a new democracy. I have met with the leading women of my own hemisphere who are working every day to promote literacy and better health care for the children in their countries. I have met women in India and Bangladesh who are taking out small loans to buy milk cows, rickshaws, thread and other materials to create a livelihood for themselves and their families. I have met doctors and nurses in Belarus and Ukraine who are trying to keep children alive in the aftermath of Chernobyl.

The great challenge of this conference is to give voice to women everywhere whose experiences go unnoticed, whose words go unheard.

Women comprise more than half the world's population. Women are 70 percent of the world's poor, and two-thirds of those who are not taught to read and write.

Women are the primary caretakers for most of the world's children and elderly. Yet much of the work we do is not valued — not by economists, not by historians, not by popular culture, not by government leaders.

At this very moment, as we sit here, women around the world are giving birth, raising children, cooking meals, washing clothes, cleaning houses, planting crops, working on assembly lines, running companies, and running countries.

Women also are dying from diseases that should have been prevented or treated; they are watching their children succumb to malnutrition caused by poverty and economic deprivation; they are being denied the right to go to school by their own fathers and brothers; they are being forced into prostitution, and they are being barred from the bank lending office and banned from the ballot box.

Those of us who have the opportunity to be here have the responsibility to speak for those who could not be here. As an American, I want to speak up for women in my own country — women who are raising children on the minimum wage, women who can't afford health care or child care, women whose lives are threatened by violence, including violence in their own homes. I want to speak up for mothers who are fighting for good schools, safe neighborhoods, clean air and clean airwaves; for older women, some of them widows, who have raised their families and now find that their skills and life experiences are not valued in the workplace; for women who are working all night as nurses, hotel clerks, and fast food chefs so that they can be at home during the day with their kids, and for women everywhere who simply don't have time to do everything they are called upon to do each day.

Speaking to you today, I speak for them, just as each of us speaks for women around the world who are denied the chance to go to school, or see a doctor, or own property, or have a say about the direction of their lives, simply because they are women.

The truth is that most women around the world work both inside and outside the home, usually by necessity. We need to understand that there is no one formula for how women should lead their lives. That is why we must respect the choices that each woman makes for herself and her family. Every woman deserves the chance to realize her God-given potential. We also must recognize that women will never gain full dignity until their human rights are respected and protected.

Our goals for this conference, to strengthen families and societies by empowering women to take greater control over their own destinies, cannot be fully achieved unless all governments — here and around the world — accept their responsibility to protect and promote internationally recognized human rights. The international community has long acknowledged — and recently affirmed at Vienna — that both women and men are entitled to a range of protections and personal freedoms, from the right of personal security to the right to determine freely the number and spacing of the children they bear. No one should be forced to remain silent for fear of religious or political persecution, arrest, abuse or torture.

Tragically, women are most often the ones whose human rights are violated. Even in the late 20th century, the rape of women continues to be used as an instrument of armed conflict. Women and children make up a large majority of the world's refugees. And when women are excluded from the political process, they become even more vulnerable to abuse.

I believe that, on the eve of a new millennium, it is time to break our silence. It is time for us to say here in Beijing, and for the world to hear, that it is no longer acceptable to discuss women's rights as separate from human rights. These abuses have continued because, for too long, the history of women has been a history of silence. Even today, there are those who are trying to silence our words. The voices of this conference and of the women at Huairou must be heard loud and clear.

It is a violation of human rights when babies are denied food, or drowned, or suffocated, or their spines broken, simply because they are born girls.

It is a violation of human rights when women and girls are sold into the slavery of prostitution.

It is a violation of human rights when women are doused with gasoline, set on fire and burned to death because their marriage dowries are deemed too small.

It is a violation of human rights when individual women are raped in their own communities and when thousands of women are subjected to rape as a tactic or prize of war.

It is a violation of human rights when a leading cause of death worldwide among women ages 14 to 44 is the violence they are subjected to in their own homes by their own relatives.

It is a violation of human rights when young girls are brutalized by the painful and degrading practice of genital mutilation.

It is a violation of human rights when women are denied the right to plan their own families, and that includes being forced to have abortions or being sterilized against their will.

If there is one message that echoes forth from this conference, let it be that human rights are women's rights. And women's rights are human rights, once and for all.

Let us not forget that among those rights are the right to speak freely, and the right to be heard. Women must enjoy the right to participate fully in the social and political lives of their countries if we want freedom and democracy to thrive and endure.

It is indefensible that many women in non-governmental organizations who wished to participate in this conference have not been able to attend — or have been prohibited from fully taking part.

Let me be clear. Freedom means the right of people to assemble, organize, and debate openly. It means respecting the views of those who may disagree with the views of their governments. It means not taking citizens away from their loved ones and jailing them, mistreating them, or denying them their freedom or dignity because of the peaceful expression of their ideas and opinions.

In my country, we recently celebrated the 75th anniversary of women's suffrage. It took 150 years after the signing of our Declaration of Independence for women to win the right to vote. It took 72 years of organized struggle on the part of many courageous women and men. It was one of America's most divisive philosophical wars. But it was also a bloodless war. Suffrage was achieved without a shot fired.

We have also been reminded, in V-J Day observances last weekend, of the good that comes when men and women join together to combat the forces of tyranny and build a better world. We have seen peace prevail in most places for a half century. We have avoided another world war.

But we have not solved older, deeply rooted problems that continue to diminish the potential of half the world's population. Now it is time to act on behalf of women everywhere. If we take bold steps to better the lives of women, we will be taking bold steps to better the lives of children and families too.

Families rely on mothers and wives for emotional support and care; families rely on women for labor in the home; and increasingly, families rely on women for income needed to raise healthy children and care for other relatives.

As long as discrimination and inequities remain so commonplace everywhere in the world — as long as girls and women are valued less, fed less, fed last, overworked, underpaid, not schooled and subjected to violence in and out of their homes — the potential of the human family to create a peaceful, prosperous world will not be realized.

Let this conference be our — and the world's — call to action. Let us heed the call so that we can create a world in which every woman is treated with respect and dignity, every boy and girl is loved and cared for equally, and every family has the hope of a strong and stable future.

That is the work before you, that is the work before all of us who have a vision of the world we want to see for our children and our grandchildren. The time is now. We must move beyond rhetoric, we must move beyond recognition of problems and work together to build that common ground we hope to see.

God's blessings on you, your work and all who will benefit from it. Godspeed and thank you very much.

[Address delivered to the United Nations Conference, Trusteeship Council Chamber, the United Nations, New York City, New York, March 14, 1995.]

It is a great personal privilege for me to join you at this Conference on Women and the United Nations. It is held in conjunction with the celebration of International Women's Day, which we celebrated, some of us together, last week in Copenhagen. It comes at a time when the role of women around the world deserves renewed attention. It is a special honor for those of us in the United States that this conference is dedicated to Eleanor Roosevelt.

Last week, when I was lucky enough to be in Copenhagen, I had the opportunity to meet with men and women around the world gathered there who are devoting their lives to the goals of eradicating poverty, protecting human rights and integrating marginalized groups into mainstream society. All of these issues disproportionately affect women and, for that reason, I and many others came away from Copenhagen even more convinced that we must work harder for ways to open opportunities to women so they may play a central role in helping find solutions for their own lives.

At a time when full economic, social and political opportunities for women too often remain an elusive goal, we should commend the United Nations for inviting serious discussion of the unique obstacles confronting women in every country, rich and poor. With the work of the world conferences in Rio, Vienna, Cairo and Copenhagen, we have helped the world elucidate the specific challenges posed to our global community. And with the U.N. Fourth World Conference on Women in Beijing on the horizon, issues historically dismissed as unimportant may now be understood in a larger global context. It is my hope that through this conference today, and the ongoing work of the United Nations, the special barriers that women face in becoming full partners in society will be viewed with greater urgency, honesty and insight.

As others have noted, it is impossible to think about the history of the United Nations, or the role of women in the United Nations, without thinking of Eleanor Roosevelt. I happen to be a great admirer of Mrs. Roosevelt, so I am doubly pleased that we are remembering her contributions today and I hope we will continue to do so as we celebrate the anniversary of the United Nations.

So much of what she accomplished as a delegate to the U.N., and throughout her life, is instructive to us today — not only as women, but because all of us as human beings at the end of the Cold War face new opportunities and challenges. It is easy at times like these, when we see so many nations confused and struggling about their own futures, wasting precious resources on building weapons of mass destruction, doing violence to basic human rights, to assume that collective global solutions exist only in the realm of fantasy. And it is equally easy to assign blame for all of the world's problems to one group of nations or another and to assume that the political and cultural divides among us are too wide to overcome. If anything, we should be reminded that every generation at every time in history faces its own special challenges. And instead of giving in to the frustration of the time or to a sense of futility we need only to think of leaders like Eleanor Roosevelt, who always for me provides inspiration and incentive to carry forward no matter what the odds.

Even before she came to the United Nations her efforts to help those in need, those less fortunate, were unparalleled. She spoke up on behalf of Japanese Americans detained in this country during World War II. The civil rights of American blacks was a special cause for her. Migrant workers, coal miners, the poor and dispossessed, anyone who did not have a voice was someone for whom she spoke. Anywhere she came across human suffering she was determined to do something about it.

When she came to the United Nations there were many who dismissed her arrival. They thought she came as a token, the widow of a great president, and she faced considerable personal challenges in undertaking the work she did. We know from various histories and from Mrs. Roosevelt's own writing that she was dismissed by a number of her fellow male delegates and, in fact, assigned to a committee where they said she could do no harm. She was assigned to the Third Committee: the Social, Cultural, and Humanitarian Committee; apparently assigned by men who had no idea what she was capable of doing. She made it from the very beginning her mission to insure that the committee, which deals so directly with the stuff of life, had a very important portfolio. We also know that she was alternately perplexed and amused by what she viewed as an obsession with rule-making among her male peers. As the men around her would sometimes argue for hours over matters that Mrs. Roosevelt felt did not deserve minutes of conversation, she would sit and knit.

It turned out to be not only a controversial job for her but one that took tremendous diplomatic skill. Among her critics was the very powerful American, John Foster Dulles, who at the end of the Assembly did finally say to her, and I quote: "I must tell you that when you were appointed I thought it terrible, and now I think your work has been fine." She wrote about her reaction to that statement in a letter home, and I quote: "So against the odds the women inch forward." I read her response with mixed feeling. Yes, I say to myself, the women inch forward. Oh dear, I say to myself, we still are inching forward and I wish we had more to show for those inches than sometimes we do.

Her role within the Assembly, although sometimes not welcome, and certainly never easy, was very important. She out-worked most of her colleagues. She did turn that Third Committee into one of the most important of the entire Assembly. She became instrumental in decisions about the fate of refugees. And she negotiated many very sensitive issues with a great deal of success.

Her greatest achievement, as we all know, was to help persuade 55 nations to sign a Bill of Human Rights, something that had never been done before. Even with her successes she was under no illusions about the capacity of this organization, or any government body or agency, to effect change on its own. The United Nations, she said soon after its founding, is "a piece of machinery and the peoples of the world have to make it work. You make it work by what you do in your own communities, by the things you build there which spread out through your representatives into your national government."

That observation by Mrs. Roosevelt holds special weight today, when all nations are grappling with a range of human problems at a time of shrinking resources and increased global competition. There is no panacea, no magic bullet that will suddenly empower women, or free people from the bondage of inhuman living conditions. Progress depends on our working together in partnership to create conditions around the world that enable women, men and children to reach their God-given potentials and flourish within their own families and societies. But today, perhaps even more than in Mrs. Roosevelt's time, there is a special urgency to helping women around the world assume their rightful places in society. That is because the fortunes of our women are inextricably tied to the fortunes of our global community. If women don't thrive the world won't thrive. At least in words, we tend to agree that women should be active participants in helping their societies meet the great challenges of this and the next century. But that can only be achieved through real concrete actions — actions that empower women through education, legal rights and protection from violence. And actions that assure women access to adequate social services, employment opportunities, political institutions and decision-making.

We know that investing in women, in their health and education, is essential to improving global prosperity. And we know that investing in women so that they can assume their rightful places in decision-making bodies is essential to continued democracy and prosperity as well. The United Nations must play a leadership role by example. Every program, policy and decision that emanates from this building directly or indirectly affects women — women as they care for children, manage households and work at their jobs. Women must be a part of the process within the United Nations as we search for answers, and women must continue to demand that their rights and opportunities be respected in nations around the world.

If one looks among Mrs. Roosevelt's great accomplishments, certainly the Bill of Human Rights continues to challenge all of us. Although international humanitarian law had been evolving before the United Nations, human rights in general and women's rights in particular were not widely recognized. On December 10, 1948, the General Assembly adopted a Universal Declaration of Human Rights and Eleanor Roosevelt played a major role in the drafting and adoption.

Now, Mrs. Roosevelt originally opposed the language in the Declaration seeking specific rights for women. But through her work in human rights she changed her position and she embraced the idea that women deserve the same rights as men, and that it must be made articulate and explicit. Because of Mrs. Roosevelt's opinion on this matter, in the fifth paragraph of that resolution the words "and women" were added. So that the paragraph reads: *Whereas the peoples of the United Nations have in the Charter reaffirmed their faith in fundamental human rights, in the dignity and worth of the human person, and in the equal rights of men and women, and have determined to promote social progress and better standards of life in larger freedom.*

Those words have enabled us to move the agenda of the United Nations forward throughout the women's conferences. They will give us the kind of platform we need in Beijing to talk about how we move forward to enable women to assume their rightful places in all societies. And they should serve as a reminder here within the United Nations that we are far from having women in enough decision-making positions in this body, either. When only 15 percent of the Secretariat are women, that is a long way from the assumption Mrs. Roosevelt had that women would be able in the years to come after 1948 to assume those positions. She was disappointed that more nations had not dispatched women to serve as delegates because she recognized that in these positions women could effectively work for equality. I think she would still be disappointed and surprised that we have not made very much progress since those early years. Certainly the United Nations — which has done such important and essential work in opening up the eyes of the world to the concept of human rights and in emphasizing the particular needs of women — should serve as an example to the rest of the world.

In paying tribute to Eleanor Roosevelt, as part of this conference, we would do well to consider her great vision, her compassion and her common-sense approach to solving very difficult human problems. For her no political obstacle was too large, no cultural gap too wide, no difference of opinion too serious to overcome. And as Ambassador Albright has reminded us, no controversy was to be avoided. One of my favorite quotations from Mrs. Roosevelt is that she often said her work was to comfort the afflicted and afflict the comfortable.

Certainly those of us, women and men together, who share the vision of the United Nations, who know the work the United Nations has done over the last 50 years, who can point to its successes, bear an even greater burden to make sure that we continue to do what we can to insure that the United Nations itself lives up to its own aspirations and that it continues to be a strong voice for all of those whose needs must be heard by the rest of the world. Thank you very much.

Tipper Gore

Tipper Gore, the wife of U.S. Vice President Al Gore, is a well-known advocate for children and actively involved with issues related to mental health and homelessness.

Gore currently serves as mental health advisor to the president. She is committed to eradicating the stigma associated with mental illness and substance abuse and continues to work toward ensuring quality, affordable mental health care.

Gore also serves as special advisor to the Interagency Council on the Homeless. She serves in a leadership capacity with representatives from 17 member agencies to improve the effective delivery of federal homeless-assistance resources and the coordination of programs at the state and local level.

In 1990, Tipper Gore founded Tennessee Voices for Children, a coalition to promote the development of services for children and youth with serious behavioral, emotional, substance abuse, or other mental health problems. She also served as co-chair of the Child Mental Health Interest Group, a nonpartisan group of congressional and administration spouses.

In 1986, Gore co-founded and chaired Families for the Homeless, a nonpartisan partnership of families that aims to raise public awareness of homeless issues. She forged a partnership with the National Mental Health Association (NMHA) to produce a major photographic exhibit entitled, "Homeless in America: A Photographic Project."

Gore also contributed to the formation of the Congressional Wives Task Force, serving as chair in 1978 and 1979. The task force sought to draw attention to the violence that children were exposed to through the media. Mrs. Gore later founded an organization to encourage the voluntary labeling of sexually explicit music lyrics and wrote a book about parenting in the media age.

Born Mary Elizabeth Aitcheson on August 19, 1948, she was nicknamed Tipper by her mother. She grew up in Arlington, Virginia. In 1970, she married Al Gore from Carthage, Tennessee. They have four children: Karenna, 22; Kristin, 18; Sarah, 16, and Albert III, 13.

Tipper Gore received a bachelor of arts degree in psychology from Boston University in 1970 and her master's degree in psychology from George Peabody College in 1975. She worked as a photographer for the *Nashville Tennessean* until her husband was elected to Congress in 1976, and remains an avid photographer. A strong proponent of regular exercise, she jogs, bikes, and enjoys roller-blading with her children.

Tipper Gore

Mental Health Advisor to the President

Tipper Gore

[Keynote Address to the American Academy of Pediatrics, Dallas, Texas, October 24, 1994.]

Thank you for the opportunity to address you today. It is a pleasure to be here in Texas this time of year, where the only people who play rougher than the Dallas cowboys are candidates for office.

It is an honor for me to speak to the people who keep our children healthy — and our parents on track.

I'm sure that for every child you diagnose with an earache or chicken pox, there's a new parent who wakes you up in the middle of the night, panicked about a 102 temperature — or mistaking baby acne for the onset of leprosy.

I've been there — more years ago than I care to admit. Our pediatrician not only treated our oldest daughter, Karenna, but he also treated a pair of young parents. Thanks to him, we were able to remain calm and level-headed when our parental instincts demanded we be hysterical.

Raising three daughters and a son has increased my love of children. That love is also professional. After getting my bachelor's and master's degrees in psychology, I intended to go into family therapy.

Then, other events altered these ambitions, but I never lost my passion for this area. Instead, I traded the therapist's office for the bully pulpit through my work with Tennessee Voices for Children, the Child Mental Health Interest Group, and now, the Clinton-Gore administration.

I was proud to make each of these choices, and for each of you, words cannot properly express how much I admire the choices you made.

In medical school, some of you may have been tempted by other fields of medicine in which the pay was higher, the prestige greater. Instead, you chose the greater good over narrow rewards. And the right values over the lesser motivations.

And that's what I'd like to talk about today: values. As far as I'm concerned, nothing has a higher value than our children. After all, why are we here on this earth if not to leave it a better place for our children?

That's what our parents did for us. And it's what we owe to the next generation.

Hubert Humphrey said:

"Each child is an adventure into a better life — an opportunity to change the old pattern and make it new."

Well, we had better change the old pattern before it's too late. Because too many children aren't being put first — they're being left behind.

Consider that children are the poorest people in America, with one in five — nearly 15 million — living below the poverty line.

Children are at special risk of homelessness, with more than 100,000 on the street, in shelters or sleeping in cars on any given night.

Children are the chief victims of the violence epidemic, with as many killed by guns between 1979 and 1991 as U.S. soldiers were killed in Vietnam — 50,000. Homicide is now the leading cause of death among inner-city children.

Children are the most vulnerable to abuse, with 2.7 million cases reported in 1991 alone. An estimated 5,000 children were killed by their care-givers.

Children are the least likely to receive treatment for mental disorders, with only 20 percent of those with problems getting care. And in many cases, inappropriate care. That leaves up to 11 million children with untreated mental illness.

Children have the greatest risk of suicide, the second-leading cause of death for those age 15-24. Five thousand young people take their lives every year.

Children suffer disproportionately from substance abuse, whether by parents, older siblings or themselves. Alcohol-related accidents are the leading cause of death among teenagers. Even 10-year-olds feel pressure to try crack and fifth-graders are sipping wine coolers, according to a *Weekly Reader* survey.

Children are too often left out of the health care system — sometimes even before they're born. One in four babies is born to a woman who had no prenatal care during the first three months of pregnancy.

As a result the U.S. has a higher rate of infant mortality and low-birth-weight babies than at least 20 other nations.

After birth, things don't get much better. One in eight children had no health insurance in 1992 — that's 8 million kids.

At a time when we are making stunning advances in technology, new drugs and new cures, it boggles the mind that children today die from preventable diseases such as measles, whooping cough, tetanus, tuberculosis and diphtheria.

Parents are trying desperately to keep their families together. But there are real, undeniable forces splintering families and piling pressures on children.

Not long ago, the primary socializing factors in a child's life were family, congregation and school. But for many kids, yet another element is instrumental in socializing them: the mass media.

The typical American child watches 30 hours of television a week — and will see 32,000 real or simulated murders by age 18.

Some popular music still glorifies brutality and violence against women, although there are warning labels now.

The result of media influences is merely one element that is contributing to nothing less than a moral breakdown in many parts of society where violence is not only tolerated, but glamorized.

And the glamorization of violence and lack of respect for human life was evidenced in the extreme by the recent murder of 5-year-old Eric Morse in a Chicago housing project. He was thrown out of a window 14 stories high by 10- and 11-year-old boys because he refused to steal candy for them and reported them to his mother.

It makes you sick to your stomach.

But this isn't just an inner-city problem.

In Davenport, Iowa, three teenage boys killed a 17-year-old girl because she refused to give them her car for a robbery.

In rural Indiana, three teenage girls lured a 12-year-old girl into a car, then beat and stabbed her before burning her alive.

In the wake of such unconscionable brutality, we leave children numb, angry, hurt and alienated, and suffering from the same symptoms that afflict children in Belfast, Beirut and Bosnia.

In short, we are faced with nothing less than a complete systemic breakdown.

How do we fight back against so many negative forces that seem beyond our control?

Not by looking for excuses and rationalizations. We don't need polemical tracts masquerading as science, like the recent book by Charles Murray and Richard Herrnstein, *The Bell Curve*. It argues that the poor have lower IQs, due largely to genetic causes. Therefore, they are destined for the bottom of the barrel no matter what we do.

This is poisonous nonsense designed to ease our guilt and justify the wholesale abandonment of tens of millions of children.

I cannot look into the shining wondering eyes of any baby and say that child was born with no potential. I know you can't, either.

We've got to fight for every child.

But we must do it intelligently and effectively.

We need to view our society holistically. You can't fix a systemic breakdown without simultaneously challenging every interconnected problem that children face.

And everyone must be part of the solution.

Government must think of children in every policy decision we make.

Parents must sacrifice to put their children first.

And every institution in society must do the same.

I'm proud to stand before you and say that the Clinton-Gore administration is doing its part.

In less than two years in office, we enacted a host of initiatives which, taken together, will help give our children a better life.

To crack down on the violence epidemic, we passed the toughest and smartest Crime Bill ever. And we enacted the Brady Law, so that guns will no longer be as easy for a kid to buy as a pack of gum down at the corner grocery store.

To fight poverty among children, we enacted the largest single measure to help low-income working families in the last 20 years — a $21 billion expansion of the Earned Income Credit.

To ease economic pressures, we cut the deficit by nearly $700 billion over five years, the largest deficit-reduction in history. Deficit reduction is a children's issue because they're the ones who will pay for our excesses.

To strengthen the American family, we enacted the Family and Medical Leave Act, so that no one will ever have to choose between keeping a job and caring for a new baby or sick relative.

To better provide for our children's health care, we enacted the Child Immunization Plan, making free pediatric vaccines available to all children who lack health insurance, or whose insurance doesn't cover them.

We fought long and hard for passage of health care reform that would have given every child health insurance, promoted preventive care and guaranteed comprehensive mental health benefits, as well.

I assure you that in the next Congress, regardless of its composition, this administration will resume the fight for health care reform with a continuing emphasis on children.

As much as we have achieved, and as far as we still have to go, government cannot solve these problems by itself. Every institution and every individual must share the responsibility and join the fight for children.

In this, pediatricians must play a special role. Your burdens are already greater than they should be. But we need you to do more.

First, we need you to keep teaching our parents — to help guide them as they raise their kids. You're every parent's personal Berry Brazelton and Penelope Leach. More than anyone, you know that kids don't come with owner's manuals. While parents often turn to their own parents for advice, family breakdown and separations lessen this resource.

We need you to help parents look out for signs of substance abuse, to teach parents how to speak frankly with children about sex, to stop teen pregnancies and the spread of sexually transmitted diseases, to warn parents about the hazards of having a gun in the house, and to coach parents on protecting their kids from violence.

In doing so, you help strengthen families, the pillar of our society and the anchor that should center every child's life.

Second, we need you to be a vital part of society's early warning system. Before children start school, the pediatric profession is the only institution outside of the family with the capacity to regularly identify children's problems: lead poisoning, malnourishment, child abuse and neglect, sexual abuse, learning and behavior disorders. If we can catch these and other problems in their early stages, we can salvage lives that would otherwise be lost. And we will save society billions of dollars in future health care costs, lost productivity, and crime.

Third, I would like to make a personal plea for you to pay special attention to the mental health of the children under your care. I urge you to look closely, to consult with mental health professionals, to pay as much attention to the brain as to every other organ in a child's body, and work to shatter the stigma of mental illness which prevents so many people of all ages from receiving needed treatment.

Finally, we need you to work closely with educators, clergy, social workers, law enforcement officers, civic leaders and elected officials to develop comprehensive, community-wide solutions to the problems facing children in your villages, towns and cities.

If we can develop effective, community-wide mental health service networks, we can treat many illnesses that are easier to cure than physical diseases... while keeping kids at home, out of institutions.

In these and other efforts, pediatricians can — and must — play a key role. Your workplace must expand beyond the office, clinic or hospital, and into the entire community.

This is a lot to ask — but our children demand no less.

And let us always remember the words of James Agee, who wrote: "In every child who is born, under no matter what circumstances, and of no matter what parents, the potentiality of the human race is born again."

Thank you very much.

Nancy Landon Kassebaum

If some people are truly "born to politics," Nancy Landon Kassebaum is near the top of the list. As the daughter of Theo Cobb Landon and Alfred M. Landon, governor of Kansas from 1933 to 1937, and a Republican presidential nominee in 1936, she grew up listening to political discussions between her father and the politicians and journalists who came to visit him. Kassebaum's family background provided an environment that spurred her intense interest in the political world.

Although her interest in politics never subsided, Kassebaum's involvement was limited during the time she raised her family on a farm in Maize, Kansas. She didn't stray too far from the political world, however, as she served as a member of the Maize School Board, Kansas Governmental Ethics Commission and the Kansas Committee for the Humanities.

In 1975, Kassebaum accepted a position in Washington as an aide to Republican Senator James Pearson of Kansas. When Pearson retired in 1978, Kassebaum joined eight other candidates in a bid for the empty Senate seat. Her forthright manner and the well-known Landon name helped propel her to victory.

Today, Kassebaum is serving her third term in the United States Senate and has risen to become the chair of the Labor and Human Resources Committee. She is known as a coalition builder in the Senate and is acknowledged as an independent thinker.

As a strong Republican voice, Kassebaum has advocated fiscal responsibility and was one of the first senators to propose a one-year, across-the-board budget freeze. Kassebaum is viewed as a moderate on social issues. She has focused efforts on improving education and reforming the health care system. She advocates greater government coordination of family and children's programs.

Foreign policy has always held a keen interest for Kassebaum. A member of the Senate Committee on Foreign Relations since 1980, she has focused much of her efforts on overhauling foreign aid programs and on African issues. Kassebaum believes that the United States must continue to take a leadership role in world affairs.

Nancy Landon Kassebaum received her bachelor of arts degree in political science from the University of Kansas. She received a master of arts degree in diplomatic history from the University of Michigan.

Nancy Landon Kassebaum

U.S. Senate
Republican, Kansas

Nancy Landon Kassebaum

[Address delivered to the African Ambassador's Forum hosted by the Carnegie Foundation, Washington, D.C., January 19, 1995.]

Thank you for the opportunity today to address this distinguished gathering of ambassadors from the nations of Africa. Let me pay tribute to the dedicated efforts of Senator Paul Simon, Senator Jim Jeffords and Congressman Harry Johnston, who in recent years have guided Congress in its approach to Africa policy. I look forward to continuing our bipartisan work.

American democracy once again renewed itself last November. A new Republican leadership now controls our national legislature and, with it, the nation's purse strings. We are at long last engaged in the belt-tightening needed to bring our federal budget under control and to secure our nation's economic future.

In this atmosphere, Americans have little tolerance for our foreign assistance programs, and foreign aid — like other government programs — will not escape the budget ax this year. The question is not *whether* we will change our foreign aid programs but *how*. And Africa — which last year received close to $2 billion in U.S. assistance, primarily for development, refugees and food aid — will be an important part of this debate.

At the same time we are approaching the threshold of a new century. The Cold War — and with it the many proxy battles fought on the African continent — is past. Many people — I am sure many in this room — worry that the U.S.-Africa relations now will suffer, not from hostility, but from neglect.

The task for those of us who care about Africa is to avoid that neglect. I am here today to call for a bold reassessment of U.S.-Africa relations, on both sides of the Atlantic. We must talk openly with each other as mature partners, all of us learning from what has succeeded — and what has failed — in the past. We must be prepared to set priorities and stick to them. Let me suggest four cornerstones that I believe are fundamental to the new foundation which, together, we must build.

First, the United States should emphasize trade development, rather than just continued aid, with the nations of Africa. Private economic ties, not flows of government money, are the basis for normal economic relations among nations. This must become increasingly true of the U.S. economic relations with Africa.

The potential for expanded ties between Africa and U.S. business is enormous — but it is still potential. Waste, corruption, political instability, and unsound economic policies too often have stifled investment and choked off growth and trade.

The result has been a continent largely left out of the mainstream of international economic prosperity. Today, for example, most nations of the world are moving forward, together, to boost world trade through the new General Agreement on Tariffs and Trade. Our people will be richer as a result. Yet, most of Africa has been left behind.

This simply cannot continue. Neither Americans nor Africans can tolerate two sets of economic rules — one for Africa and one for the rest of the world. The plain truth is that the state-run economies that failed in eastern Europe, in the former Soviet Union, and in many nations of Latin America and the Pacific have failed in Africa as well. And the liberal economic and political reforms that are transforming those regions can also transform Africa.

For my part, I intend to work more closely with the American business community to increase awareness and understanding of Africa. As chairman of the Subcommittee on African Affairs, I intend to call my first hearing to review the investment climate in Africa and the effectiveness of federal programs designed to promote the private economic ties of American companies abroad.

Second, we should strengthen our commitment to basic teaching and training in Africa. As I have found in this country, there is no substitute for strong technical education. Basic skills are the gateway to future economic growth and to progress toward civil societies. We should focus on training more of Africa's promising young people in Africa, which increases the odds that they will use their new skills to help their communities.

Third, we should work together to construct basic infrastructure for the African continent as a whole. Just as the nations of North America have bound themselves together through a network of telecommunications, roads, rail and air routes, and just as the Europeans have done so, I believe Africa must as well. Ours is a modern world, and much economic growth today is predicated on access to the tools of instant communications. Likewise, there is a great need for a far-reaching, efficient transportation network to carry the commerce which is the lifeblood of economic progress.

Fourth, I believe the United States should redouble its commitment to a strong diplomatic engagement in Africa. America has friends and foes in Africa, as we do in every other part of the world. We will not embrace those who engage in activities such as terrorism, narcotics trafficking or rampant corruption.

Diplomacy is an instrument of low cost but potentially enormous yield. We are all better off when we can reason together. Diplomacy has contributed to peace in Mozambique, and it has brought us renewed hope for peace in Angola.

Sixteen African nations are involved in some sort of civil conflict. These conflicts have produced some 6 million refugees and 17 million displaced persons. And far too much of America's economic aid to Africa goes to relieve the consequences of civil conflict. I want to invest in something more lasting. From Liberia to Somalia, from Sudan to Zaire to Nigeria, there is an essential role for America's diplomatic strength. But we must not delude ourselves into believing we can change Africa from Washington.

Americans will continue to support humanitarian assistance, and we will also continue to support efforts to conserve Africa's greatest natural resources. Of Africa's many attributes, nothing engages the attention of Americans more than the majestic wildlife and great natural beauty of your continent.

We stand ready to help with the great political, economic and social reforms that must occur. But these fundamental changes in the structure of African society must come primarily from African initiatives. There is encouraging work under way by the Organization of African Unity, by East Africa's Intergovernmental Association on Drought and Development, and by the Economic Community of West African States. These African initiatives are a first step.

Africa has many success stories to tell — in Benin, Namibia, Botswana, Malawi and Uganda. Nearly two-thirds of African countries are at some stage of democratic transition. Similarly heartening are the efforts to create economic unions. Nowhere is this progress more encouraging than among the nations of the Southern African Development Community. The world is closely watching your efforts to bind your economies and move forward together. Only your leadership can bring future progress.

I must be frank — the new foundation I propose will inevitably lead to a re-ordering of U.S. priorities in Africa.

Those countries which pursue failed economic policies, which continue closed political systems, which oppress their people and fail to provide a stable environment for investment — will naturally fall in priority for the United States. This is as it should be.

By contrast, those African countries which aggressively pursue market-oriented economic policies, which are committed to economic and political reform, and which are pursuing or maintaining stable political systems can expect closer ties with the United States. We place great value on the basic elements of good governance and civil society — transparent decision-making, an independent judiciary, basic human rights, and free and fair elections.

These are ideas which I hope will be thoroughly discussed. They would lead to real changes in U.S. relations with the countries of Africa. But if we are not bold, the consequences for the future of U.S.-Africa relations will be severe.

The greatness of the African continent has not yet begun to be realized. You, in Africa, will have to provide much of the leadership — America, as your partner, offers our support. The responsibility to lay a bold, new foundation is ours alone.

[Address delivered to the Institute for the Study of Dipolmacy, Georgetown University, Washington, D.C., March 21, 1995.]

I am pleased to be here this morning to discuss with you the questions of multilateral security and the future of peacekeeping. As all of you know, there is a great deal going on in Congress. We are still intensely and appropriately focused on a long domestic agenda.

However, this forum is both timely and necessary as the debate begins in earnest on the future of our foreign policy. I have just left a hearing of the Senate Committee on Foreign Relations, which is intended to delve into the very topics outlined in your agenda this morning.

We are now deep in the wilderness of the post-Cold War era. There are few signs or guideposts to tell us which way to proceed. President Bush's New World Order had become rampant disorder and President Clinton's "assertive multilateralism" has evolved into a timid globalism.

Some would say that we have reached a fork in the road — if there were any road. There is not. We are blazing a trail into unknown and potentially very dangerous territory. The basic structures of the Cold War — the North Atlantic Treaty Organization and other security guarantees — no longer rest on the solid foundation of global deadlock between matched superpowers. However frightening that foundation may have been at times, it was at least well-known and clearly understood.

I am not among those who pine for the good old days of the Cold War. Nor am I one who sees a world where America stands as the sole superpower with unilateral ability to do as we please wherever it might please us.

During the Cold War, America was always first among equals. We were not always successful in setting the course, but we were never ignored. American leadership has responded in mixed ways to the changed relationships. President Clinton seems to view the world as a fuzzy international debate club where we can all get together, talk things over, and work it out. Some Republican leaders view the world as a hostile, treacherous conspiracy that requires the United States to adopt a porcupine strategy — touch me and I'll jab you.

Neither of these views offers America a realistic or even useful road map into the difficult terrain of the next century. Fuzzy multilateralism is a dead end if it is not grounded in core values and beliefs. Prickly unilateralism is almost guaranteed to drive away those who might rally to our cause in times we most need friends and allies. Our current debate between so-called internationalists and isolationists is, in reality, a sterile, pointless exercise that is disconnected from the real world in which we not only live but can and must thrive.

What is strikingly absent from this debate is any sense of American self-confidence. One side says that we cannot do anything without the rest of the world behind us. The other responds that the world will not follow our lead, and we must go it alone. As always, the truth lies somewhere between these extremes.

The end of the Cold War, which I think we can rightly claim as a victory, is a startling achievement for any time and place in human history. But we seem to feel no vigor, no exhilaration in this success. Instead we seem drained, indecisive, uncertain. The unknown and unknowable challenges ahead seem daunting in their very mystery, and it is seductive to think we can find a safe corner from which to observe.

The isolationists' corner offers a long and valued tradition that predates our Republic. In fact, America itself was the original isolationists' refuge for escape from the Old World. Our founders instinctively feared and resisted foreign entanglements, and in the process of honoring that tradition, we have avoided much mischief and many heartaches.

The internationalists' corner offers a more recent but no less valued hallmark of American policy. The end of World War II left us as the paramount power and the unquestioned leader of the West. Much like today, we hemmed and hawed in the period immediately after the war. But we rose to the challenges of Soviet expansionism and forged alliances that spanned the globe.

I have no doubt about our ability and our will to meet each and every challenge that may come in the years ahead. We will do so not on either of the paths we are now debating but in the uniquely American mixture they have always provided. We will meld our isolationist tradition with our unavoidable place in the wider world.

We will be, in short, the United States of America — with no ambitions to take that which is not ours and no willingness to surrender that which rightfully belongs to us. We seek no empire and will fight any empire that is raised against us.

Our aversion to empires of any stripe is not a matter of political convenience or intellectual speculation. It is in fact a defining element of our national character. It is joined indelibly to a second characteristic that defines America: an unshakable belief in the rule of law. These two beliefs — the rejection of empire abroad and the enshrinement of law at home — are important in our foreign policy. They are the bedrock of our character.

As we make our way into the great transition that is now reshaping the world around us, we Americans must remember who we are and what we are about. My sole fear in this period is not that we will misunderstand the world beyond our borders — the world has a way of imposing its facts upon us — but that we will misunderstand ourselves.

We have done so before — most prominently perhaps in the aftermath of World War I when we rejected the League of Nations and tried to hide behind our ocean ramparts. We may do so again, in a period where risk-free solutions and short-term success are allowed to overrule clear thinking.

Most Americans understand the real challenge that lies ahead. They know that the hard questions are not true or false but multiple choice. They know that American interests overlap and intertwine with the interests of other nations, just as our personal interests must always be balanced with the interests of fellow Americans. Most Americans know that our real task now is to find the right balance between working with others and going it alone.

I have spent a lot of time here outlining the current debate over foreign policy. I have done so in the belief that we cannot create a post-Cold War security structure unless we begin on a solid foundation and unless we know what tools are available for the work.

I am not suggesting that our mission should be to recreate miniature Americas in every nation on the planet. But I believe strongly that our national interest lies in reducing the power and reach of dictators, strong men, and one-party governments wherever they may exist. By working to make such governments responsive and responsible to their own people — by nurturing and spreading the rule of law — we join in a common cause toward mutual goals not only with friends and allies but with those who need and are needed by us.

This is not the work of one Congress or even a two-term president of either party. It is a work that will require decades of patient, relentless diplomacy. It will require a thoughtful blend of military muscle, economic might, and skillful persuasion. It will require the work of many nations, including some that do not now exist. It will require a sorting out of the type of response necessary for humanitarian relief, or for national security concerns, or for peacekeeping.

We now have most of the tools necessary to this task. We have unmatched military forces tied to strong and effective allies and we possess extraordinary economic, political and diplomatic power. The two missing ingredients seem to be a clear sense of national purpose and the will to proceed — in short, strong leadership to point the way — and an international body that can help focus and apply all of the resources at hand.

The current status of the United Nations, however, is both ironic and alarming. If we did not now have the United Nations, we would be forced to invent it. But if we could invent the U.N., we would not invent the one we now have.

I consider myself a solid friend and a strong advocate for the United Nations. I believe it can and must play a critical role in the challenges that lie ahead. The U.N. is the one body that can focus both international attention and resources on the issues before us. Unfortunately, it seems increasingly irrelevant and ineffective.

The superpower deadlock of the Cold War years prevented the United Nations from ever achieving its true potential. American and Soviet vetoes in the Security Council blocked any decisive move. This deadlock also allowed the U.N. to develop a number of bad habits, such as a bloated bureaucracy more intent on advancing the goals of the U.N. personnel than the cause of world peace. Lines of authority are confused, blurred and duplicated into nonexistence. Basic missions and activities have ballooned into ponderous, unwieldy exercises that produce mountains of paper and little, if any, real results.

That may seem like a harsh assessment but remember that it is offered as a friend of the United Nations. The U.N.'s detractors are far less generous or forgiving.

The reality is that the United Nations as it exists today is not sustainable. The legitimate excuses for inaction created by the Cold War are gone. The United Nations must begin to fulfill its true potential or it will be left to suffocate in its endless debates over meaningless issues, or become a road show traveling from summit to summit.

I am aware that there are serious efforts under way to reform the U.N. I applaud all such efforts, but I fear they lack both the boldness and the urgency necessary to the task. Rearranging deck chairs will not do. We need a decisive change of course that produces a smaller, more focused, more efficient United Nations with clearly defined missions.

We do not have such a United Nations today. We cannot succeed without that kind of U.N. in the years ahead. If we fail to insist on radical change at the U.N. or in assisting such reform, we will squander a large part of the opportunity that now exists for creating a more stable, peaceful, prosperous world in the 21st century.

That would be a tragedy beyond measure, just as the League of Nations was in its own time.

Dianne Feinstein

U.S. Senator Dianne Feinstein of California has made a career of taking on tough battles.

Since her election to the Senate in 1992, Feinstein has written legislation that initially was given little chance of passage, but which won approval in Congress and was signed into law by President Clinton. Such legislation includes a ban on manufacture, sale and possession of semiautomatic military combat weapons. It also includes the California Desert Protection Act, which incorporates more than 3 million acres of rolling sand dunes, extinct volcanoes and pristine mountain ranges into two national parks — Joshua Tree and Death Valley — and one national preserve — the East Mojave.

Re-elected in 1994 to her first full six-year term (her first election to the Senate filled the unexpired term left by Pete Wilson, who had been elected California governor), Feinstein serves on three Senate committees: Judiciary, Foreign Relations and Senate Rules and Administration.

Feinstein began her career fighting crime, a goal she has maintained through her military assault weapons ban and support of the national Crime Bill. As a member of the California Women's Parole Board from 1960 to 1966, she reviewed sentences and determined whether to parole women who had been convicted of felonies and sent to prison in California. In 1968 she was a member of the San Francisco Committee on Crime.

In 1969, Feinstein was elected to the San Francisco Board of Supervisors with more votes than any other candidate, thereby making her the president of the city's legislative body. She was re-elected for two additional terms, serving three terms as board president. In November of 1978, in the aftermath of the assassinations of Mayor George Moscone and board colleague Harvey Milk, Feinstein became mayor of San Francisco. In the following year she was elected to the first of two four-year terms.

Feinstein's career has been a series of firsts. In 1969, she was the first woman to be elected president of the San Francisco Board of Supervisors. In 1984, she was among the first women to be openly considered for the Democratic nomination for vice president of the United States, and in 1990 she became the Democratic candidate for California governor, the first woman to be nominated for that position by a major party.

34 *American Women Speak*

Dianne Feinstein

U.S. Senate
Democrat, California

Dianne Feinstein

[The following are proceedings and debates of the 103rd Congress, First Session, July 29, 1993.]

Weapons of war have no place on America's streets.

Every day, another terrible tragedy reinforces something about which I deeply believe — weapons of war have no place on the streets of our communities. Semiautomatic assault weapons — which can empty 50- to 100-round magazines of ammunition within seconds and without warning — are turning America's streets into war zones.

Epitaph headlines convey this modern-day horror: "Arsenals Amassed in L.A. County;" "Gunman Slays 2, Wounds 3, Outside CIA;" "Fear Stalks L.A. Streets;" "At least 9 Die in California Shooting."

It is time to stop the continuing bloodshed on our streets.

Just a few weeks ago — on my birthday, as a matter of fact — right here in Washington, D.C., a young gunman stood on a hill 40 yards from a pool where young children played. He opened fire and unleashed up to 14 shots from what police believe was a semiautomatic pistol. Six children were wounded. Yet — thankfully — none was killed.

I then returned home on July 1 to the news that a lone gunman — carrying two semiautomatic weapons, a pistol and 500 rounds of 9mm ammunition — walked into the Pettit & Martin law firm located high in one of San Francisco's premier office buildings. He, too, opened fire. This time he killed eight people and wounded six. It just so happened that, as he was going from one floor to another on the stairwell, an employee pulled the fire alarm which locked the doors. He was locked into the stairwell, where he killed himself.

I then picked up a newspaper while still in California and read that in Oakland, a 3-year-old boy, playing with his godmother's 5-year-old daughter, pulled a semiautomatic assault weapon from under her bed, fired it three times, and shot the 5-year-old with a MAC 11 semiautomatic pistol. His playmate suffered bullet wounds in both of her legs and a bullet grazed her temple. Luckily, by the grace of God, she still lives today and is expected to survive.

But California's past is increasingly dotted by such incidents.

I remember well when James Huberty walked into a McDonald's in San Ysidro, California, in 1984 with a Uzi. Twenty-one people were killed. Nineteen people were wounded. I also remember well when, in 1989, an unstable drifter with an assault weapon modeled after an AK-47 walked onto a Stockton schoolyard in Northern California and fired 106 rounds of ammunition. Five children were killed. Twenty-nine children were injured.

What, in the past, have been shocking episodes, however, are now becoming the norm. The almost daily slaughter of drive-by shootings and the reign of terror caused by assault weapons on the streets of major cities across the nation has to be stopped.

Calamities such as those in Stockton and San Ysidro led California to become the first state in the Union to ban assault weapon sales in 1989. Yet, without a national ban on these weapons, local and state initiatives are meaningless, because gun buyers can simply cross state lines and purchase their weapons of choice. And today, these fast-firing guns are the weapons favored by gang members involved in drive-by shootings, and organized criminals.

Nationally, it is estimated that there are about 1 million such weapons in circulation. In California, my state, there are an estimated 300,000 to 600,000 assault weapons on our streets and in our communities. That is 30 to 60 percent of the 1 million weapons available throughout our nation.

Yes, it is true that guns do not fire themselves. Nor, however, do they thrust themselves into the hands of the distraught, deranged and disaffected. They have to be bought or stolen. And today in all but four states — California, New Jersey, Connecticut, and Hawaii — they can be bought, legally, over the counter.

Yes, over the counter. That is how Gian Luigi Ferri got the TEC-DC9s that he used to kill eight people at 101 California Street in San Francisco.

A California resident for less than a year, Mr. Ferri did what thousands of people in my state do — he crossed the state line to buy a weapon of choice. A former Nevada resident, Ferri used a still-valid driver's license to buy one Uzi-like gun in Las Vegas, waited the requisite three days, and returned to pick it up.

Two weeks later, he purchased an identical weapon at another Las Vegas gunshop. And he returned to California with two TEC-DC9s in his possession.

Ferri's assault weapon of choice — the Miami-made Intratec TEC-DC9 — is typical of its ilk. It is relatively cheap, easily concealed, holds 30- or 50-bullet magazines, and can fire as fast as a demented killer, gang member, drug dealer, or assassin can squeeze the trigger. Most sickening of all, Ferri's guns sported a special spring-loaded hellfire switch — legal even in California — that allowed them to be fired, for all practical purposes, as fast as a machine gun.

Ironically, Ferri could have bought the gun he was after in California.

This photograph shows a semiautomatic assault pistol that has been banned by the state since 1989 — and yet the gun used by Ferri is simply a copycat version of this weapon. And this copycat version is still legal today, almost anywhere across America.

Ferri killed eight people shortly after he entered the building at 101 California Street. But he shattered the lives of scores more.

I would like to read portions of one letter written to President Clinton by Stephen Sposato, with whom I have talked on the telephone. He is the husband of a young wife who was the mother of his 10-month-old child. He was the first victim of Gian Luigi Ferri. He said:

> *Recently, my beloved wife, Jody, died a brutal and unnecessary death when bullets from a semiautomatic weapon took her innocent life in San Francisco. Her right to live has been violated. Our 10-month-old daughter's right to her mother has been violated. My right to have this family has been violated. It is indeed a tragedy when a person can purchase and use a weapon that takes the lives of so many people and alters the lives of so many others, especially my dear late wife, Jody, and my daughter Meghan Marie.*
>
> *The laws that permit the sale and use of semiautomatic weapons in the United States must change.*

Mr. President, what further evidence than this tragedy do we need to classify semiautomatic weapons as those of mass destruction?

Mr. President, I think the answer to this question is painfully obvious. The time for action is now.

The time to impose a national ban on the sale, manufacture, and possession of all semiautomatic weapons of war that flood our streets is at hand.

When imported assault rifles were banned by the Bush administration in 1989, the number of these weapons traced to crimes by the Bureau of Alcohol, Tobacco and Firearms declined by 40 percent, while the number of crimes traced to domestic assault weapons increased. Let me provide one example of how readily these weapons are available today.

The Street Sweeper — also known as the Striker 12 — is a shotgun designed and developed in South Africa as a military and police riot gun. With its revolving-cylinder magazine, it can fire 12-gauge shotgun shells in less than three seconds.

Importation of this weapon was banned in 1989 — yet the manufacturer found a way around the ban. Today it is produced domestically by two companies. Even worse, the gun can be purchased through the mail.

This chart shows a flyer — provided to me by an official with the government of the District of Columbia — that boldly claims:

> *Our customers know us as the company that fought ATF for three years to allow import of this superior weapon for them. * * * Appeal after appeal BATF said no. * * * Did we let BATF stop us delivering the goods to our customers? No! They've gotten theirs. * * * Now you can get yours!*

And the gun is sold through the mail, legally, for $540.

The free flow of assault weapons across state lines and through the mail — and the resulting nationwide proliferation of such weapons — reinforces the need for strong, clear federal laws banning all assault weapons.

When weapons of war are available over the counter, the federal government has no way of keeping them out of the wrong hands.

More than 10,000 guns were stolen in Los Angeles County alone in 1992. Only 200 of these have been recovered. Nearly 15,000 guns were stolen elsewhere in California. And in one case, at a gun store located on 77th Street in south Los Angeles, looters made off with 1,150 guns — including nearly 600 semiautomatic weapons.

I am especially concerned that teenagers who want a weapon know today exactly where to find one. A stunning survey released last week by the Joyce Foundation found that 59 percent of all children in 6th through 12th grade said they could get a handgun if they wanted one. Thirty-six percent said they could get one within an hour. Only 30 percent of the more than 2,500 students surveyed said they feel safe going to and from school.

It is time to stop the bloodshed, Mr. President. It is time to ban assault weapons.

Two pieces of legislation address this very real problem — and two of our distinguished colleagues — Mr. DeConcini and Mr. Metzenbaum — have fought for years to ban these weapons.

Mr. DeConcini's bill — the Anti-drug Assault Weapons Limitation Act of 1993 — would ban the import, possession, sale, and transfer of 14 semiautomatic assault weapons, such as: the AK-47 used in the Stockton schoolyard shooting in 1989; the MAC-11 used just last week by the innocent 3-year-old playing in Oakland; and the Street Sweeper and Striker 12 sold so easily through the mail.

I am sad to say, however, that manufacturers have already demonstrated how they can get around this bill: by immediately making and marketing copycat versions. The four states, including California, that have imposed statewide bans on assault weapons have seen this disturbing trend — gun manufacturers will develop copycat models, sometimes just changing the name of the gun to avoid well-intentioned state laws.

Senator Metzenbaum's bill, however, attacks this problem head-on. Not only would 20 semiautomatic weapons be banned by name — but the attorney general would be required to add weapons to the prohibited list that manifested two or more defined characteristics or functions that make assault weapons so deadly. Characteristics like detachable magazines that hold more than 10 rounds of ammunition or the ability to accept a grenade launcher or bayonet.

That will ensure that copycat models — versions of these lethal weapons — will be quickly and permanently banned. I intend to add an amendment that would exempt semiautomatic bolt action shotguns and bona fide hunting rifles whose clips do not exceed three rounds, so that hunting weapons are exempt from this legislation. Under the Metzenbaum bill, for example, both the TEC-9 and the copycat TEC-DC9 used to kill eight people at 101 California Street would be banned once and for all.

Senate Bill 653 also targets the ammunition clips that are readily available today — magazines with more than 10 rounds of ammunition would be banned.

When Ferri walked into 101 California Street, he carried with him eight 50-round clips and four 30-round magazines — more than 500 rounds of 9-mm ammunition. That volume of ammunition can be legally purchased at any gun store in America today.

I sincerely believe it is time for this bill — the Semiautomatic Assault Weapons Violence Prevention Act of 1993 — to become law.

Next Tuesday, the Senate Judiciary Committee will hold a hearing on assault weapons. Family members of the victims whose lives were lost in the San Francisco shooting, public officials concerned about rising crime, and law enforcement officers will testify. Hopefully, this will result in the committee sending the legislation to the floor of the Senate for consideration.

I was astonished to learn recently, Mr. President, that no major gun control legislation has passed Congress in the last quarter century. Not since 1968, following the assassinations of Rev. Dr. Martin Luther King Jr. and Senator Robert F. Kennedy, has Congress been willing to restrict the flow of guns to our streets.

In that quarter century, we have witnessed dramatically rising crime and rising fear. According to figures by the FBI, the number of people killed by guns increased 76 percent from 1968 to 1991, the last year for which figures were available.

This Congress will soon have before it an omnibus crime bill. There is no better vehicle for imposing a ban on the sale and possession of semiautomatic weapons — and the high-capacity ammunition magazines often associated with these fast-loading and fast-firing guns.

The public clearly wants such legislation. Consider the answer to three separate questions in recent polls:

Asked: "Would you favor a law banning the manufacture, sale and possession of semiautomatic assault guns, such as the AK-47?" Sixty-six percent said "yes;" only 30 percent said "no."

Asked: "Do you favor stricter gun control laws? Sixty-eight percent said "yes;" only 29 percent said "no."

Asked: "In general, do you feel that the laws covering the sale of firearms should be more strict, less strict, or kept as they are now?" Seventy percent said they should be more strict; only 4 percent said less strict.

I urge every American who is concerned about the flood of weapons on our streets to write to Washington, D.C. Write the president, the attorney general, your senator, and your representative in Congress.

Voice your concern, express your fears. Only with the loud push of public opinion will this legislation ever, I believe, become law.

It really comes down to blood or guts. Those are the options that Congress must choose between very soon: Between the blood of innocent, terrified people, of children, of those mowed down at work, at meals, at play by semiautomatic assault weapons, or the guts to ban these insidious weapons of war from our streets once and for all.

The people of my state and the victims of horrendous crimes, such as the murderous rampage at 101 California Street, ask for your support. It is time to stand firm and outlaw these weapons of war.

Thank you, Mr. President.

[Dialogue between Senator Feinstein and Senator Larry Craig, Republican of Idaho, as excerpted from the Congressional Record, November 9, 1993.]

Craig: *The senator from California wants to ban those kinds of weapons that were used by James Huberty in San Ysidro, California. He's the fellow that went into the McDonald's restaurant and killed 19 people. What did he go in there with? He went in there with an Uzi, and she wants to ban those, a 9-millimeter carbine, a conventional 9-millimeter pistol, and a 12-gauge model 12 shotgun. Where did the bulk of the killing come from? Eleven people were killed in the first minute and a half with the shotgun. Huberty used the shotgun first. He killed most of the people with the shotgun that the senator from Tennessee is going hunting with this weekend.*

That's the reality check for tonight. She is banning the gun that was used second and third. Reality check says that any gun, if the intent of those who hold it is to wreak havoc on society, it can become an assault weapon. Now, that's the whole of the text, and I could go on and on with these kinds of issues.

So, the gentle lady from California needs to become a little bit more familiar with firearms and their deadly characteristics. I say that —

Feinstein: *Will the senator yield for a point of personal privilege for a moment, please?*

Craig: *Yes, certainly.*

Feinstein: *I am quite familiar with firearms. I became mayor as a product of assassination. I found my assassinated colleague and put a finger through a bullet hole trying to get (a pulse in his wrist). I proposed gun control legislation in San Francisco. I went through a recall on the basis of it. I was trained in the shooting of a firearm when I had terrorist attacks, with a bomb at my house, when my husband was dying, when I had windows shot out. Senator, I know something about what firearms can do.*

Kay Bailey Hutchison

Kay Bailey Hutchison became the first woman from Texas to be elected to the United States Senate after claiming more than two-thirds of the vote in a special runoff election on June 5, 1993. Hutchison was re-elected in November 1994 to a full, six-year term in the Senate. Although a junior member of the Senate, Hutchison serves on several key committees: Armed Services, Commerce, Science and Transportation, Small Business, and Intelligence.

On the Armed Services Committee, Senator Hutchison has advocated stronger support for United States military personnel and their families, and for increased readiness of our armed forces. After 18 months on the Armed Services Committee, she became the first woman to serve on the Senate Select Committee on Intelligence. Hutchison has also been named a deputy majority whip and is co-chair of the Senate Republican Regulatory Reform Task Force.

Prior to her election to the U.S. Senate, Hutchison served as Texas state treasurer from 1990-1993, where she cut her budget more than any other statewide elected official, while increasing returns on state investments to $1 billion for the first time in the state's history. She led the fight against a state income tax in 1991 and successfully recommended that the Legislature limit debt in Texas.

President George Bush tapped Hutchison to serve as temporary co-chair of the 1992 Republican National Convention, where she delivered a widely noted welcoming speech.

As a member of the Texas Legislature from 1973 to 1976, representing a Houston district, Hutchison earned outstanding leadership awards from numerous state and local organizations. In 1976 she was appointed vice chair of the National Transportation Safety Board by President Gerald Ford.

After moving to Dallas in 1978, Hutchison was named senior vice president and general counsel of Republic Bank Corp. She later co-founded Fidelity National Bank of Dallas and owned McCraw Candies, Inc., a manufacturing company with national distribution. She sold the company in 1988. Before running for public office, she worked as a political and legal affairs correspondent for KPRC-TV in Houston.

Kay Bailey Hutchison is a graduate of the University of Texas at Austin and the University of Texas School of Law. She and her husband fund two scholarships at the University of Texas and one at Southern Methodist University School of Law.

Kay Bailey Hutchison

U.S. Senate
Republican, Texas

Kay Bailey Hutchison

[Speech delivered to World Economic Forum, Davos, Switzerland, February 28, 1995.]

As you know, this past November the Republican Party captured control of both chambers of Congress: the Senate and the House of Representatives. In nearly 500 separate contests for state governors, senators, and representatives, many Democrats were defeated, but not a single Republican running for re-election lost.

After nearly half a century of believing that our federal government had the capability, indeed the obligation, to solve all problems and cure all inequities, Americans have returned to a view of themselves and their government that emphasizes personal responsibility, opportunity, and independence. This is a lasting change, one that will certainly endure to the turn of the century and beyond.

In domestic policy, this means we should no longer seek to write laws and regulations in Washington to govern every aspect of daily life.

In the realm of foreign policy, policies supported by both Democrats and Republicans have advanced democracy and helped to make the world today a freer and more stable place. In fact, all of the major foreign policy goals set out by the Truman and Eisenhower administrations have been fulfilled in the Reagan and Bush administrations.

The recent elections do not foreshadow American isolationism, as some reports have suggested. The United States will remain a leader and we will continue to play a major role in world affairs.

But the American people are demanding that we apply a consistent, rational standard to our commitments: the government of the United States should commit its full energy and power only to those issues and problems in which there is a demonstrable national interest, for which we can define success in concrete terms, and in which we can expect to succeed.

The world remains a dangerous place. There are still acute threats to our security and peace that must be met. The Persian Gulf War demonstrated the folly of imagining that evil and aggression have been banished from the globe.

Among America's alliances, none is more important than the Atlantic Alliance. But lately there have been sharp words exchanged among friends over how best to address the situation in Bosnia.

We must not allow our disagreements over Bosnia to further divide the most successful security alliance in history. To quote Winston Churchill, "There is one thing worse than fighting with allies and that is fighting without them." The National Atlantic Treaty

Organization (NATO) is a pivotal framework for guaranteeing peace and stability in Europe, and I want to emphasize that America's commitment to NATO will remain strong.

American interests in the East are no less important. In the past decade, the East Asia and Pacific region has surpassed Western Europe to become the largest regional trading partner of the United States. Again, America has played a key role in this growth and I believe the growth will continue.

The most acute issue in the Pacific Rim, of course, is North Korea's apparent determination to develop nuclear weapons. While the new Congress will not halt implementation of the nuclear framework agreement, we are gravely concerned and have every intention of attempting to strengthen it. We think all responsible nations should join in requiring North Korea to verify that it is not making nuclear weapons.

We will solicit full disclosure from the Clinton administration to ensure that the terms of the current agreement do not actually increase the nuclear threat — or the conventional threat — to our forces and the forces of South Korea. The only prudent course for the United States is to strengthen its military presence in the region.

Although the president and the Congress are divided on many issues, we now agree that primary responsibility for our foreign policy resides — and ought to reside — in the executive branch of government.

Neither this Congress nor the American people will tolerate the delegation of our commander-in-chief's authority to the United Nations — or to any other multilateral organization. And we will take action in the new Congress to make our position on this issue understood.

The Republican Congress will ask hard questions before we agree to support troop deployments on multinational missions. This is not a retreat from our obligations or a desire for isolation. Let me be clear: we currently shoulder a disproportionate burden of the costs of peacekeeping operations, and we provide a large share of the military equipment required. I believe we will continue to provide funds and logistics support but our military participation should no longer be taken for granted.

We also understand that we must work to keep our country strong economically, as well as militarily. I again quote Winston Churchill, who said, "Peace is our aim; strength is the only way of getting it."

Economic strength is just as important as military might. Expanded commerce among nations is the path to growth and prosperity, and America will continue to stand for free trade. Lower tariffs and barriers under the North American Free Trade Agreement (NAFTA) and the Uruguay Round will stimulate our economy and those of other nations.

But protectionism is not the only barrier to global prosperity. Developed nations — and many developing nations — must encourage entrepreneurs.

American business has spent the last five years cutting costs and improving productivity. But more must be done. The Republican Congress will attempt to help business grow and create new jobs by cutting the private sector's largest cost — taxes and regulations. If we follow the General Agreement on Tariffs and Trade (GATT) tariff cuts with cuts in taxes and regulations, we will create the best environment for world trade ever, and will raise living standards throughout the world. The United States is working to do this — but there is much to be done:

> **Repeal Regulations.** Regulation is on the rise in all industrialized countries. In the United States, complying with government regulations cost $580 billion in 1993. Many economists believe burdensome regulations cost even more in European countries.
>
> I'm co-chairing a task force of United States senators that is exposing regulators who have gotten out of control, and we're working to rein them in and repeal their regulatory regimes.
>
> **Reduce Taxes.** Tax rates in developed countries are among the highest in the world. Germany, Italy, Japan, Great Britain, and the United States all have top income tax rates of 40 percent or more. Hong Kong has a top rate of 25 percent, and a flat corporate tax of 17 percent. It is not surprising that Hong Kong also has one of the highest growth rates in the world.

But the global economy — especially with global capital markets — is a two-edged sword. We cannot have the benefits of global trade and capital investment without being affected by economic instability among our customers, partners, or investors.

For the United States, a crippling downturn in the Mexican economy would mean fewer exports — and a sharp reduction in the anticipated growth promised by the North American Free Trade Agreement. We have taken some immediate steps to bolster the peso. But agreeing on how to restore confidence and give Mexico long-term security will be difficult.

Finally, many people are wondering whether the new Congress can balance the federal budget. It is a daunting task that has confounded previous Congresses for years. It will take several years, but we can do it, with the help of both parties — and with the backing of the American people.

To summarize, Republicans will seek to return America to the constitutional model of a limited government — protecting, but not directing, a strong society of free individuals.

We will neither withdraw from the world, nor settle every dispute. We will remain strong, we will remain committed to our alliances, and we will remain engaged.

Christine Todd Whitman

Christine Todd Whitman was elected the 50th governor of New Jersey on November 2, 1993, becoming the first woman in the state's history to win its highest elective office.

During the years prior to her election as governor, Whitman was no stranger to an active and productive public life. She served on a variety of boards, commissions and volunteer bodies. Among them were the Community Foundation of New Jersey, the National Council on Crime and Delinquency, the New Jersey Advisory Council on Corrections and the North Jersey Transportation Coordinating Council.

In 1982, Whitman was elected to the Somerset County Board of Chosen Freeholders, which oversees the financial administration of the county government. She was re-elected in 1985 as the top vote-getter on the ticket. She served on the board for five years, including terms as director and deputy director. She was involved in the opening of the county's first homeless shelter and first halfway house for alcoholic male teenagers, as well as the construction of the county's modern courthouse, which was completed on time and under budget.

In 1988, Governor Tom Kean appointed Whitman to serve as president of the New Jersey Board of Public Utilities (BPU). During her two years administering that board, she fought to keep utility rates low and won high marks for instituting an ethics code for the board.

Whitman resigned from the BPU in 1990 to run as a Republican for the U.S. Senate, challenging Senator Bill Bradley, New Jersey's Democratic incumbent. She received 49 percent of the vote. Following her narrow defeat, Whitman remained active in public affairs, writing a newspaper column and hosting a radio talk show. She also formed the Committee for an Affordable New Jersey to support legislative candidates and speak out on issues. During those three years, she led the campaign that took her to her current position as governor of New Jersey.

Whitman earned a bachelor of arts degree in government from Wheaton College in Norton, Massachusetts, in 1968.

Christine Todd Whitman

Governor of New Jersey
Republican

Christine Todd Whitman

[Remarks delivered in Trenton, New Jersey, March 6, 1995.]

Good morning.

From the outset of my administration, I have talked about the need to develop an urban strategy to turn our cities around.

Not a repeat of costly big-government programs that have failed to make our cities safer, or more prosperous, or more livable.

But rather a new, sensible strategy that puts neighborhoods and communities in charge of their own destiny.

The key to a successful urban strategy is partnership. Communities and local governments working together as partners in developing a plan to revitalize their city. The partnership expands to state government, and then to the private sector.

That's the philosophy behind our urban strategy.

And we are putting that philosophy into practice right here in Trenton.

Our Urban Coordinating Council (UCC), made up of the members of my Cabinet, has begun taking action on specific requests made by the people of Trenton.

The UCC is ending the era of confusing, uncoordinated, and inaccessible state programs. Through the UCC, the state for the first time is serving cities in a more integrated and coordinated way.

And it's working because of leaders like Mayor Doug Palmer, the concerned citizens of the Canal Banks Area, and the Trenton Enterprise Initiative.

Let me offer a few examples of how it works.

The Canal Banks neighborhood has no supermarket. The city expressed an interest in developing a small grocery store like the one on Lalor Street.

Now, the Economic Development Authority (EDA) will explore with the city various ways to assist in financing the supermarket.

As another example:

The city complained to us that it takes the Department of Health as long as three years to turn data around — which makes it extremely difficult to track and assess social service programs.

In response to this complaint, the Department of Health will create a special task force to improve data flow between the state and Trenton on such indicators as infant mortality. We expect to clean up this system by the end of 1995.

Finally, we are taking a holistic approach to job training.

Our partners in Trenton told us that Mercer County Vocational Schools are difficult to reach by public transportation. They suggested a local facility would boost participation in job training programs. We agreed.

Not only will we establish a local job skills center, but the Department or Labor will also install an Automated Labor Exchange (ALEX) terminal in the proposed skill center or in another appropriate spot to provide easier neighborhood access to job opportunities. And by July 1, 1995, the Department of Labor will reserve $200,000 in customized training funds to help businesses in these neighborhoods employ local residents.

In short, we are forming a partnership with the people of Canal Banks and the city of Trenton to improve the quality of life in the neighborhood.

We are doing the same in Camden, Elizabeth, and Asbury Park, the other cities that have joined with Trenton to launch our urban strategy.

I would like to take a moment to acknowledge the mayors of these cities: Doug Palmer of Trenton, Arnold Webster of Camden, Chris Bollwage of Elizabeth. Patricia Candiano of Asbury Park could not be here today.

These mayors, and the citizens they represent, are all making our urban strategy succeed.

In Elizabeth, the major immediate concern was for quality affordable housing. Now the Department of Community Affairs is working to give Elizabeth and the other cities priority consideration to receive balanced housing funding and low-income housing tax credits.

In Camden, the emphasis is a program to help low-income minorities acquire skills to own and operate their own businesses. So the EDA has responded by expanding their successful Entrepreneurial Training Institute to Camden.

For the residents of Asbury Park, a place for their children to play in safety was of paramount importance. Smith Barney took up our invitation to adopt a neighborhood and offered to build a playground in Asbury Park — proving that local and state partnership can promote private-sector investment.

Ron Ferrelli, an executive vice president for Smith Barney's New Jersey Division, has joined us today. Ron, on behalf of the neighborhood Smith Barney adopted and those you may adopt in the future, I would like to thank Smith Barney for its generosity.

I would also like to take this opportunity to thank the community colleges for offering to support our urban initiative in innovative and tangible ways. They are perfectly suited to help urban residents acquire and improve job skills, promote small- and minority-business development, and provide mentoring and job placement for high school students.

For our urban strategy to truly succeed, we are calling on everyone — community groups, businesses, clergy, educators, local officials, police, and charitable foundations — to work together. The power that comes from these partnerships will revitalize our cities neighborhood by neighborhood.

A community-centered strategy has never been attempted as a matter of state policy. Individual citizens, groups, or businesses have generally been on their own, while state government went about drafting programs that it thought were the answer to the cities' problems.

Over the last 10 years the state has invested more than $7 billion in these four cities alone. Clearly, these dollars have not solved the problems.

I am confident we will get better results by putting people and neighborhoods at the heart of everything we do. We will enable the cities to find their place — as centers of commerce, culture, government or research or simply as home to New Jerseyans who prefer the urban lifestyle.

We won't solve all the problems of our urban centers overnight. But we can start today to commit ourselves to a new way of working together that will form the basis for real change for the future.

Thank you.

Ann Richards

Ann W. Richards' tenure as the 45th governor of Texas, from 1990 through 1994, was the result of a lifetime of public service — as a teacher, a civil rights activist, a worker for women's rights, Travis County commissioner, and state treasurer.

In 1976, Richards was recruited to run for office and defeated a three-term incumbent for a seat on the Travis County Commissioners Court at a time when, she recalls, "Texas was not noticeably hospitable to the notion that a woman could handle that kind of responsibility."

Six years later, Richards ran again — this time for state treasurer. She won with more votes than any other statewide candidate on the ballot, becoming the first woman elected to statewide office in more than 50 years. In 1986, she was re-elected without opposition. During her eight years as state treasurer, Richards oversaw the installment of leading technology in the treasurer's office, and pioneered banking and investment practices that earned taxpayers more non-tax revenue than all the other treasurers in the history of Texas combined — more than $2 billion.

In 1988, Richards came to national political attention when she delivered the keynote address to the Democratic National Convention. Within two years, on November 6, 1990, she was elected governor of Texas.

As governor, Richards led Texas toward economic health. In 1992, more jobs were created in Texas than in any other state in the Union. As the state's top salesperson, Richards helped recruit and retain new manufacturing facilities and new expanded corporate facilities that brought one out of every three jobs created in the United States in 1992 to Texas.

Richards spearheaded the fight against crime, supporting the tripling of the minimum sentence for capital murder, curbing the early release of violent offenders, and supervising the rewriting of the Texas penal code to insure the state's most violent criminals stayed behind bars. Richards addressed the problem of repeat offenders by creating prison substance-abuse programs to stop the cycle of crime where it often starts: with drug and alcohol addiction. As a result of the state's policies, the crime rate in Texas declined for the first time in 10 years.

Since Richards' defeat in her try for a second term as governor, she is beginning a new life away from public office. She opened an Austin, Texas, office for a Washington, D.C., law firm, Verner, Liipfert, Bernhard, McPherson & Hand. Additionally, she makes periodic speeches across the country and sits on selected corporate boards.

Ann Richards

Governor of Texas
(1990-1994)
Democrat

Ann Richards

[Speech delivered at the Mexico-United States Border Governors' Conference, February 22, 1991.]

*B*uenas tardes.

Primeramente les quiero dar gracias por su generosa hospitalidad a mi estimable colega el Honorable Gobernador de Sonora, el distinguido licenciado Rodolfo Félix Valdez — muchísimas gracias.

Estimados gobernadores, fue un gran honor para mi tener un representante del Presidente Salinas de Gortari y a los cuatro gobernadores de los estados fronterizos con Tejas en mi inauguración.

Entre Tejas y México existe un nexo eterno entre todos los que viven en ambos lados de la frontera.

Es lazo de alma, de corazón, hecho fuerte por una cultura común, una herencia común y una creencia en la dignidad de cada persona.

As governors we share a determination to help our citizens make the most of their lives — to encourage the commerce and economic growth that will bring prosperity to our families and a better future to our children.

We in Texas appreciate the economic potential of the partnership between our two countries.

In 1989, Texas exported $9.8 billion worth of goods to Mexico, an increase of nearly 20 percent over the previous year.

And as Dr. Jaime Serra Puche told us at breakfast, the port of Houston handles more Mexican merchandise than all Mexican ports combined.

The *maquiladores* [border textile factories] have offered sources of economic opportunities on both sides of our border.

We in Texas know that the successful conclusion of the free trade agreement negotiations will have a tremendous impact on our economy, because we will be literally at the geographic center of a hemispheric trade zone 25 percent larger than the European economic community.

Market share can no longer be viewed as a parochial activity; it will be multinational in nature if we are to succeed in world competition.

The negotiations on the agreement are complex. But we have great faith in the ability of our governments to work cooperatively — and in the ability of our people to overcome any obstacles that may exist.

We have working examples of that ability now.

As mentioned by Gobernador Villareal-Guerra, the United States, Mexico and Texas have developed a cooperative agreement to finance and construct a wastewater treatment plant in Nuevo Laredo, Tamaulipas, that will help reduce the pollutants in the Río Grande.

Texas and Coahuila have devised an arrangement to fight crime on both sides of our border by exchanging scientific and technical information relating to the investigation of crimes, by coordinating efforts to fight drug trafficking, and by agreeing to the return of stolen property crossing the border.

Three of the Mexican border states are working with Texas to promote tourism by developing the "two nation vacation" and we believe that development of the historic corridor along el Camino Del Río Bravo will enhance those efforts.

Our education exchanges, as discussed by Ambassador Negroponte, are tremendously successful.

So we know that there are great possibilities for more cooperative ventures and we know no matter how carefully crafted a free trade agreement is, the burden of ensuring its success will rest primarily on those of us along the border.

We must work together to develop the infrastructure — the roads and bridges, ports and railroads — that tie us together. Without infrastructure that allows us to capitalize on the agreement, it will be little more than words on a page. In Texas, we have seen more international bridges and border crossings approved and constructed in the last five years than we had seen in the previous 20.

That improvement is the outgrowth of the work of these conferences. And we must do more of it. The issues discussed here are not only of regional importance; they are hemispheric. Our discussions, our actions, our successes in the areas of trade, environment, health, education and transportation will ultimately affect all the citizens of our states and our nations.

We in Texas are mindful of our responsibilities and the wonderful opportunities which are ahead.

You have my pledge that we will work with energy, optimism and honesty as we undertake the task before us.

Our border with Mexico is not the back door to the United States, it is the front door to a new world of trade.

As it is said in *México y Tejas: ya es tiempo de ponerle manos a la obra.*

Thank you.

[Speech delivered at Girls' State, June 18, 1991.]

I hope you all remember Alice's encounter with the Cheshire Cat during her adventures in Wonderland.

"Would you tell me, please, which way I ought to go from here?" asked Alice.

"That depends a good deal on where you want to get to," said the cat.

"I don't much care where —" said Alice.

"Then it doesn't matter which way you go," said the cat.

"— so long as I get to somewhere," said Alice.

"Oh, you're sure to do that," said the cat, "if you only walk long enough."

Well, isn't that the truth? We're all going somewhere whether we choose our destination or not.

Over 40 years ago, I sat where you sit today.

And if you had told me that I would one day return to Girls' State as the governor of Texas, I would not have believed you.

But during that summer so long ago, I developed what would be a lifelong interest in politics and government. It never seriously occurred to me that I would seek political office myself.

After high school, my life followed a pattern pretty much like the one mapped out for girls of my time.

I never had a plan or grand scheme. I just let life happen to me the way I had always been told it was supposed to.

I went to college and thrived on debate and history classes.

I married my high school sweetheart and set about the business of being the perfect wife and mother — which, of course, included being the perfect lover, nurse, housekeeper, chauffeur, psychiatrist, interior decorator, travel agent, chef, and social director.

And I was good at it.

It was not hard to continue an interest in politics.

And, for years, I participated in the women's auxiliary brand of politics.

I licked and stuffed envelopes, staffed the phone banks, went door to door, helped set up the fund raisers — and watched the men debate policy.

And when I finally ran for my first political office, I did so at least partially because my husband didn't want to run and suggested me as a substitute.

That decision to run for county commissioner 14 years ago was, truth be told, the first time I had had a serious talk with myself about where I was going.

Like Alice, I had always been eager to arrive somewhere — but I had never taken the time to choose my destination.

Experience and instinct told me that my life would be dramatically changed by my decision — and I was right.

But I knew that if I let the opportunity pass, I would always wonder what might have been — would always wonder what playing it safe had cost me.

So I ran.

Because, you see, it is not so much a matter of choosing your final destination as it is deciding that you will travel your own course, that you will take responsibility for your own life.

When I was at Girls' State, we seemed to have fewer options.

We all assumed we would marry after we had gone to college and learned to teach or nurse or work in an office.

After all, we needed something to do until Prince Charming entered the scene, and our mothers warned us to get a degree just in case we faced the awful prospect of having to take care of ourselves.

There were precious few role models for those of us who had a gnawing feeling that there must certainly be more to life than baking the perfect pie crust and getting our laundry whiter than white.

The history books showed us no pictures of strong women leading independent lives; public life held no guiding examples.

Oh, there was the occasional fluke occurrence, like Amelia Earhart, who dazzled the nation as a daring pilot — only to disappear at sea.

But not many of us were ready to go the way Amelia went — and we saw little to ease the loneliness of feeling yourself a freak because your mind told you there must surely be more for women to do.

Now there are more of us for you to see and learn from — and learn from both our success and failures.

Now most of you have some hint that if Prince Charming comes along, he's likely to be riding a Honda and expecting you to make the payments.

Now it seems that you can be whatever you want to be. You have nothing but options.

The great myth for women in my youth was safety and security — a lifetime of protection earned by giving yourself totally to caring for others.

In your time, the myth is superwoman — the woman who can work 12 hours a day toward achieving distinction in her profession and still manage to create a home life like the Bill Cosby Show.

The real world doesn't run like the Huxtable household and, I suspect, your family doesn't either.

In the real world, half of all marriages end in divorce, and over 70 percent of divorced women find themselves slipping toward poverty.

In the real world, less than 20 percent of our families fit my old stereotype where Dad goes off to earn the paycheck and Mom stays home and takes care of the kids.

The vast majority of American families are headed by parents who both work or mothers trying to rear their kids pretty much by themselves.

The world where most of us live is made up of men and women who live from paycheck to paycheck, who fret about finding decent day care, who struggle constantly to keep a sense of personal balance.

In the real world, when Mama works, she's not usually an architect or a lawyer.

She's more likely to find herself in an office job earning a salary just above the poverty level.

We still earn only about 60 cents for every dollar earned by the men.

And women in professions are no exception: on average women professionals earn $160 less per week than men in the same profession.

And the real world doesn't make it easy for us to have children and work. Sixty percent of us find we have no guaranteed leave policy when it comes time for us to give birth.

Don't get me wrong: we have made tremendous gains in the last 15 years or so — and your options are the evidence of it.

But true equality — social, economic, and political — is still somewhere in the distance for us.

In the real world you study here — the world of politics and power — our gains are persistent but slow.

Nationwide, we hold just over 15 percent of elected statewide positions — and about the same percentage of legislative and city council seats.

We are 7 percent of the mayors and 5 percent of Congress.

We have three women governors.

And, because we are at Girls' State, it is that real political world that I want you to think about.

Until recently, women have tended to leave the politics to our menfolk.

But that was a terrible mistake because we failed in our responsibility.

You see, we women really are different from the men — and we bring a different perspective to public service.

We have been the caretakers, the supporters, the nurses, the cheerleaders, the fence-menders, the peacemakers.

Now we are beginning to see that our difference is our greatest strength — and the strength which is so desperately needed in the real world.

Unlike the Cheshire Cat, we lead best by helping others find their way.

But we cannot help unless we take responsibility for ourselves.

It is essential that we educate ourselves, prepare to support others financially — and determine to move out of Wonderland and into a real world of our own making.

I hope that one day, 30 or 40 years from now, one of you will stand up here on the dais — as governor of Texas or president of the United States — and you'll be able to start by saying:

A long time ago, a woman named Ann Richards stood up here and told us that we could change our world for the better by taking on our fair share of responsibility.

And we have.

Patricia Schroeder

When political talk turns to outspoken, independent Democrats in Congress, one name surfaces with regularity — Patricia Scott Schroeder, the U.S. representative from Colorado.

Patricia Schroeder was first elected to Congress in 1972 and has been re-elected 11 times. She is currently the longest-serving woman in the House of Representatives. Schroeder is a member of the House Judiciary Committee, where she is a ranking Democratic member on the Subcommittee on Courts and Intellectual Property. Schroeder is also a member of the National Security Committee, where she sits on the Subcommittee on Military Research and Development.

As chair of the House Armed Services Research and Technology Subcommittee, Schroeder led efforts on conversion of defense research and technology for civilian purposes, including law enforcement and women's health. Schroeder began the first comprehensive effort to assess the costs and benefits of our mutual defense alliances, and has called on our allies to contribute a greater share of resources for their own defense.

Representative Schroeder is equally vocal and productive about such issues as women's economic equity, health, educational opportunities, constitutional rights, and policies that affect children, women and families. During the 1993-1994 session of Congress, Schroeder authored and helped make law the Violence Against Women Act, which strengthens efforts by law enforcement agencies, prosecutors, and victim-service organizations to combat violence against women. Her National Child Protection Act gives child-care providers and youth service groups access to information on convicted child abusers, and her Child Support Responsibility Act prevents, among other things, non-custodial parents from avoiding their child support obligations. In 1989, she authored a book outlining a family policy agenda for the 21st century: *Champion of the Great American Family* (Random House).

Representative Schroeder graduated magna cum laude in 1961 from the University of Minnesota, where she was a member of the Phi Beta Kappa honor society. She received her juris doctor degree from Harvard Law School in 1964, and practiced law in Denver.

Patricia Schroeder

U.S. House of Representatives
Democrat, Colorado

Patricia Schroeder

[Speech delivered before Harvard Law School, Cambridge, Massachusetts, October 1, 1993.]

Nothing comes without a fight. Nothing. That is true for men and women. And the fights are not only tough, but in many cases, close. History has been determined by fights where one vote made the difference.

In 1776, a difference of one vote made English, rather than German, America's language. In 1868, a difference of one vote saved President Andrew Jackson from impeachment. And in Greece over a thousand years ago, the Church Synod decided by one vote that women were human beings rather than animals.

Even as we celebrate 40 years of women being at Harvard Law School, we need to remind ourselves of the fight it took to get us here. Not once, but twice, in 1899 and 1915, Harvard's governing corporation took up and decided against having women in the law school.

Electing the first woman president will be no less a fight. But before we can seriously discuss it, we need to analyze what stands in the way of women achieving the ultimate in political power. I believe our biggest obstacle lies in the fact that women do not share a universal definition of what it means to be equal in American society.

For women, fights to change the law have been ever tougher, primarily because, while women gave their lives to fight for their country, for the abolition of slavery, and for children's rights, they have been uncomfortable about fighting for themselves.

Women's issues have an added complexity because we — women and men alike — are ambivalent about women's role in society.

Just when it seems that society is comfortable with women as independent, powerful, and equal, there's a backlash. In the 1970s the Supreme Court upheld women's right to an abortion. Congress enacted laws to protect women from discriminatory practices. And our popular culture, whether it was through advertising, movies or magazines, encouraged the independent woman to take charge of her life.

In the 1980s, however, things began to slowly change. Despite the fact that support for the Equal Rights Amendment (ERA) reached a high-water mark in 1981, it was defeated in 1982. Reagan and the Republicans got rid of the women's rights plank in their platform. The religious conservatives, who held that women moving into the work force were undermining the American family, began to rise in power. And women who were making it in society were doing so by imitating men.

This backlash was prompted by only the possibility that women might gain full equality. Women are vulnerable to a backlash because there is no consensus of what equality for women under the law means. Consequently, women are vulnerable to shifting cultural standards. The media knows that if they get 10 women in a room and ask them, "What do women want?" they will probably get 10 different answers.

Why? Four reasons:

First, women's argument for the right to vote was based upon the premise that women were more moral than men and that superior morality was based upon our unique biological differences — the ability to bear and nurture children. So basically we got the vote because one, we were different; two, we were pure; and three, with the power of our superior moral ability we could clean up the process. Nineteenth-century women paraded as paragons of femininity. Women, they said, should be released from the home to fulfill a higher role — to be society's moral guardians.

You reap what you sow. We convinced the male power brokers so well that they instituted a body of law set out to encourage, protect, and basically institutionalize that moral superiority. Policymakers pounced on that admission of "difference" and produced legislation designed to "protect" women. They protected us from entering and practicing the law, but not from scrubbing floors.

Second, about the time Harvard Law School allowed women to enroll, women were included in the 1964 Civil Rights Act as an afterthought, without the thoughtful public debate that usually accompanies such a major societal change.

Third, the Supreme Court has never given the same constitutional protection to equal rights as they have to civil rights. In fact, it wasn't until 1971, in Reed v. Reed, over 100 years after the adoption of the 14th Amendment, that the court found a state law discriminating against women to be unconstitutional. Since 1971, the court has heard over 50 cases involving sex-based challenges under the equal protection clause to state and federal laws relating to hiring, promotion, maternity leave, pension rights, seniority and disability insurance. And while the court has made it clear that stereotypes of men and women's roles will not have weight in its decisions, it does not give women the same constitutional protections that it gives men.

Consequently we really have no legal equality standard for sex. It is as if we built a house on stilts instead of concrete blocks. We survive the storms, but barely. And if the big one hits, we could be gone.

Fourth, not only do women not have a fixed reference point in the law by which to measure their standing under the law and in society, we also have shifting cultural standards as to the proper role of women in society.

About seven years ago, Jill Abramson and Barbara Franklin wrote *Where They Are Now*, a book which followed 70 women from the Harvard Law Class of 1974 — some of whom I am sure are here tonight — through a decade. I think their findings crystallize why women and men are ambivalent about the risks, the costs, and the value of women defining and attaining equality in our society.

Abramson and Franklin found that 10 years after graduation, there was a dramatic difference between the men of Harvard '74 and the women from the same class. Twenty-five percent of women made partner in that time, compared to 51 percent of the men. Their book is a series of profiles and interviews with the women, especially women on the partnership track, to find out why that discrepancy existed. Women from the class of '74 were in the job market about the time the superwoman model became prevalent. In the 1980s it seemed as if every magazine you picked up had articles about women who ran a household, raised children, jogged three miles a day, held a high-power job, and had a dynamite recipe for cookies.

It isn't a surprise that many women in the class of '74 who went to work in law firms with the goal of attaining partnership opted out of the rat race, for a variety of reasons. Some decided the cost of attaining partnership wasn't worth it. Others felt they didn't have enough flexibility to raise their families or have any type of personal life. Still others found that once they were in a firm, the firm didn't really know what to do with them or how to deal with them.

For many the bottom-line equation was, can I be sure if I invest eight or nine years of my life in the pursuit of partner, that being a woman won't be held against me? Eight or nine years is a huge bet when you have limited time on your biological clock. And how will the stereotype of women play against me? Will I be seen as too aggressive, too sexual, too reticent, too girlish or too pushy? When I decide to have a child, will I be viewed as not caring about my career? These concerns being played out by the class of '74 were also being played out by women everywhere. There is work and there is family. How do women merge the two, without giving up on either, in a way where they don't die from stress?

Our society's ambivalence towards women's roles in society, fueled by a culture that daily bombards women with images, messages, polls, ideas, trends, statistics, and opinions about what they should be, has not made our efforts to decide who we are and what we want any easier. Our ambivalence is a market — for some, an industry. It's the bread and butter of our popular culture. Playing on women's ambivalence about who we are and what we want is big business in America. It's time to put that ambivalence aside and pursue a lasting standard of equality that recognizes women's differences but not to the detriment of our ability to contribute to our society. We can and will do it.

We've won many advancements over the last two centuries, but there is much to be done. There are many fights on the horizon. Let me mention two.

Health Care: Although we still lack health care reform, we are finally talking about the issue in this country. As Congress decides what it means — from financing to benefits — women have to be active in that debate.

From mammograms to contraceptives to abortion, women must decide what we need for comprehensive and seamless health care. We cannot let politicians determine what women want and need for comprehensive health care. It's time for women and their doctors, based on good medical research, to run the show. Women deserve health care that is medically necessary, not politically necessary.

Family-Friendly Workplace: By that I mean not only a workplace that accommodates workers with families, but also one that doesn't penalize women who have families. We need benefits for part-time work, an infrastructure of care that allows us to fulfill our duties as parents to our children and children of our parents, and an ethic in the workplace that instills in workers that they can be both a good worker and a good family member.

If you haven't enlisted in at least one of these fights, you are shirking your duty. Don't let the statistics of how far women have come in society lull you into inaction. We need to use the incredible *gravitas* and talent in this room to retire the charts of statistics and make equality a comfort zone for women and a reality in the law.

Corrine Brown

Congresswoman Corrine Brown of Florida was elected to the U.S. House of Representative in November 1992. She serves on the Transportation and Infrastructure Committee and the Committee on Veterans' Affairs. In addition, Brown is an active member of the Congressional Black Caucus, the Caucus on Women's Issues, the Older Americans Caucus, the Congressional Sunbelt Caucus, the Congressional Space Caucus, and the Congressional Fire Services Caucus.

Brown is an advocate for economic development, education and senior citizens' rights. She has introduced legislation to create more health care facilities for veterans and has co-sponsored measures to reduce crime, making her one of the most productive freshman members of Congress.

A native of Jacksonville, Florida, Brown served in the Florida House of Representatives for 10 years, from 1982 through 1992. During her decade of service, she was the first woman elected chairperson of the Duval County Legislative Delegation. Brown also served as a consultant to the Governor's Committee on Aging and was appointed to represent women of Florida on the Manpower Training Council.

Brown attended Florida Agricultural and Mechanical University, where she earned bachelor of science and master's degrees. She also received an education specialist degree from the University of Florida. Brown has been a faculty member at Florida Community College at Jacksonville, the University of Florida and Edward Waters College.

Corrine Brown

U.S. House of Representatives
Democrat, Florida

Corrine Brown

[Speech delivered at Unity Day Program, Mt. Zion AME Church,
Ocala, Florida, July 29, 1994.]

Thank you so much for inviting me to join you this morning for your Unity Day Program at Mt. Zion AME Church.

Our young people are our most important resource for the future. I hope that through community work like yours, our young people can learn from the triumphs of historic black leaders that they can accomplish their dreams.

Just look at the history that's been made: for the first time in over 120 years, an African-American represents this district in Washington. These changes could not have occurred without the groundwork laid by great African-Americans like Thurgood Marshall and Arthur Ashe, and Floridians like Dr. Mary McLeod Bethune, Zora Neale Hurston, James Weldon Johnson, Gwen Sawyer Cherry and Mary Singleton.

I hope our young people realize what an exciting future they have ahead of them. With hard work, they can accomplish amazing things. History was made with the 103rd Congress. Sixteen new African-American members were seated in the House of Representatives and one African-American senator, Carol Mosely-Braun, was seated, expanding the number of Congressional Black Caucus members to 40, the largest ever. There are now 54 women, 19 Hispanics, nine Asians, and one American-Indian. This is the highest number of minorities to ever serve in the history of the United States Congress. I, and others, would not have the privilege of serving in Washington if it were not for the courage and sacrifice of those great leaders who led the way before us.

Let me tell you a little bit about Florida's first black member of Congress. Josiah Wells was first elected to the House of Representatives in 1879, but his election was challenged and he lost his seat after only two months in office. However, he had already been re-elected to a new term by then. Believe it or not, his next victorious election was challenged after ballots were burned in a courthouse fire. And thus ended the congressional career of Florida's first black representative.

Once Reconstruction began, 21 black congressmen were elected from the South between 1870 to 1901. However, after 1901, when Jim Crow tightened his grip, no black person was elected to Congress from the South for over 70 years. As we celebrate Black History Month this year, it is more timely than ever to look at what happened to black representation during Reconstruction. This period may seem like ancient history, but what happened then seems to be happening all over again. I have to ask you here in Ocala what I asked my colleagues in Washington: Are African-Americans any better prepared for the reconstruction of the

1990s than we were for the first Reconstruction when the Congressional Black Caucus shrunk from 21 to zero in 30 years?

As you may be aware, the Voting Rights Bus Tour recently traveled through North Florida to try to spread the word about the threats to our rights to fair representation. I, and others in the Congressional Black Caucus, Rev. Jesse Jackson and the National Rainbow Coalition wanted to educate people in our communities across the South about the recent court challenges to minority districts growing out of last summer's U.S. Supreme Court decision, *Shaw v. Reno*. Since that case was handed down, years of good case law that sought to expand voting rights for minorities were tossed upside-down. Now, court challenges have been filed against minority districts in North Carolina, Louisiana, Georgia, Texas, and right here in Florida.

On Monday, July 18, the U.S. District Court in Tallahassee denied a motion to stop the upcoming elections this fall and allowed the Department of Justice to intervene in this case. I am very encouraged by the District Court's ruling. I have strongly supported the Florida attorney general's efforts to have this case dismissed as groundless and frivolous; the court's latest ruling demonstrates the weakness of the plaintiff's case. I am also encouraged that the U.S. Department of Justice has been allowed to intervene in the case on behalf of preserving the 3rd Congressional District as it is now drawn.

The plaintiffs filed their lawsuit in January, but they waited until now, two months before the primary elections, to ask for an injunction based on an erroneous interpretation of the Supreme Court's decision in *DeGrandy*. The Supreme Court affirmed the existing Florida map, not invalidated it as the plaintiffs claimed. The court-approved reapportionment and redistricting plans for Florida resulted in more African-American, Hispanic and female representation than had existed before the 1992 reapportionment and redistricting trials. As a result of those trials, which I was a party to, along with Mr. DeGrandy and others, Florida has made important gains in minority representation.

Just this last week, in Georgia, those who want to send us to the back of the political bus are trying to throw out the minority district represented by Congresswoman Cynthia McKinny. Unfortunately, Gary Franks, congressman from Connecticut, traveled to Savannah to urge the court to throw out our hard-fought district. I was present in the courtroom and couldn't believe my ears to hear Mr. Franks' attacks on our districts. It is offensive that someone from Connecticut, who is unfamiliar with voting rights problems in the South, would attack our hard-won gains caused by the Voting Rights Act.

The Voting Rights Act was enacted because people who should have been represented were not represented. Too many have died for us to allow a few frightened individuals to steal back long-overdue minority-access districts like ours. What matters most is not what the district looks like, but who is served — those who have been left out. The shape of a district is not mentioned in the Constitution but representation is — it's guaranteed.

Now that finally in some states like North Carolina, Georgia and Florida, the minority delegation in Congress begins to reflect the minority population in these states, the shapes of minority-represented districts are being attacked. These attacks are from the good old boys from the bad old days who are trying to roll back the clock and send minorities to the back of the political bus. We can't let that happen.

The Congressional Black Caucus recently met with President Clinton, who issued a strong public statement that "inclusion of all Americans in the political process is not a luxury, it is central to our future as the world's most vibrant democracy." If the courts don't do the right thing, we will introduce legislation to recapture the spirit of the Voting Rights Act.

We've also got to stop the explosion of violence in our communities. Let me tell you a bit about what's going on in Washington. The House recently passed the Crime Bill. Although it is not a perfect bill, I supported the Crime Bill because it begins to address the root causes of crime. It addresses prevention through community policing, and youth employment skills, midnight sports, Boys and Girls Clubs in public housing facilities and other measures that will help our young people choose a productive life instead of a life of crime — especially for our at-risk youth. This bill will also crack down on domestic violence and other crimes against women. I voted against an amendment that would strike racial justice language in the bill. The Congressional Black Caucus supported the language in the bill, known as the Racial Justice Act, which would prevent execution of prisoners who could demonstrate that their death sentence was imposed because of racial discrimination.

Of course, the real difference won't come through legislation alone — it must come at home with families teaching our children to respect themselves and respect others, teaching them the difference between right and wrong. The real difference must come in our neighborhoods by remembering the African proverb: "It takes a mother to bear a child, but it takes a whole village to raise that child."

What we really need to concentrate on are the root causes of crime. We need to concentrate on prevention, not on building more prisons. Did you know that the incarceration rate in inner cities is already more than 3,000 per 100,000? That's 10 times worse than South Africa. What are we doing with our prisoners while they are in prison? Are they improving their education? Are they learning job skills so that they can compete for a job once they get our? Are they learning personal skills so they can keep a job and reunite their families once they get out?

I can't stress how important prevention is. It begins with prenatal care for our women, it requires full immunizations for every child in this country. It requires an Even Start and a complete Head Start for every eligible child. We can't just get our disadvantaged children to first grade and then, without any other special attention, expect that by 11th or 12th grade they'll magically be ready to go to college. We've got to have full funding for our schools, not budget cuts in education, so that our neediest kids have a real opportunity to make the most of their time in our schools. Rev. Jesse Jackson recently visited New York City and toured many of the city's schools. He saw over 800 broken windows in the New York City schools and made a very important point — there are probably no broken windows in the jails in New York. If we made the most of our resources while our children are in school now, they might never end up in jail!

Friends and families of our children must do something to break the code of silence about the breakdown of family and spiritual values. All parents must do more to value our children so they know that they're somebody special! Parents and families need to be able to teach our children right from wrong by example and by teaching them discipline and self-control. Parents need to be better role models for our children and fight for what they need in our communities, such as preventive measures, like education, family support programs, jobs for our young people, and programs to keep children safe and off the streets when they are not in school. Each of us can do a great deal to help youngsters learn about their responsibilities to their communities, and help them learn the value of hard work instead of glamorous short cuts like drugs and gangs.

I'll close my Unity Program remarks today by saying united we stand and divided we fall. The Black Caucus has been able to accomplish quite a lot because the 40 of us have stood together. Just think what we could do if this country's 30 million African-Americans and our friends worked together — Oh, what a force we would be!

Again, thank you for inviting me and I look forward to working with each of you to make our communities what they once were, something we can be proud of.

[Editors' note: Representative Cynthia McKinney was elected to represent the 11th district in Georgia for the current 104th Congress and is expected to serve out her term, although a court could order a special election once new district lines are drawn. McKinney has not ruled out running for office in a newly drawn district.]

Tillie K. Fowler

Congresswoman Tillie Fowler's political career began in 1967, when she accepted a position as legislative assistant to U.S. Representative Robert G. Stephens Jr. of Georgia, a Democrat. In 1970 she left Capitol Hill for the Nixon White House, working for a year and a half as counsel in the Office of Consumer Affairs. In 1971, she switched party affiliations from Democrat to Republican.

While taking time out from her professional career to raise a family, Fowler followed a familiar pattern for women who want to remain active in community service. She joined and participated in a number of charitable and benevolent institutions, including the American Red Cross and the Junior League in Jacksonville, Florida.

Community involvement led Fowler to run for the Jacksonville City Council. She was elected in 1985 and served for seven years. From 1989 to 1990 she was president of the Council, both the first woman and the first Republican to serve in this capacity.

Elected to the U.S. House of Representatives in 1992 as part of the largest freshman class since World War II, Fowler hit the ground running as a strong advocate of congressional reform and term limits, pledging to serve a maximum of four terms. She was elected co-chair of the Freshman Republican Task Force on Reform, and her tenure in that position was highlighted by the passage of several reform amendments and the first-ever House hearings on term limits legislation. She also was elected to serve as one of two freshman members on the Republican Policy Committee.

Fowler was re-elected without opposition in November 1994. She is the only Republican woman member of the House National Security Committee. Fowler, a deputy Republican whip, also serves on the Transportation and Infrastructure Committee and is a member of the National Security Caucus.

Tillie K. Fowler

U.S. House of Representatives
Republican, Florida

Tillie K. Fowler

[Speech delivered to the Society of Military Comptrollers in
Jacksonville, Florida, May 16, 1994.]

The past few months have seen the world celebrating the epic push to victory begun by the Allies on the beaches of Normandy in June of 1944. Yet the resurgence of interest in D-Day has dimmed the recollection of some of World War II's less successful campaigns — for example, the doomed delaying action fought by American and Filipino troops on the Bataan Peninsula.

Sent to defeat the Japanese without resources or reinforcements by a nation too weak to rescue them when it became clear they could not accomplish their mission, these troops were either mercilessly slaughtered or survived only to suffer through a forced march and imprisonment and torture in POW camps. After the First World War, the U.S. had given in to isolationist sentiment and cut defense spending to the bone. The Japanese attack on Pearl Harbor not only devastated the Pacific Fleet but left our nation scrambling to put together adequate personnel and equipment to fight what almost immediately became a two-front war.

Ten years after the Bataan Death March, we dispatched 540 troops to stop the Communists from invading South Korea. They were equipped with 10 WW II bazookas, which had already proven inadequate against German tanks, and had only six rounds of anti-tank ammunition — one-third of the stockpile in the Far East. Although we sent in reinforcements, our troops paid in blood for their lack of equipment and preparation, with 54,246 dead and 200,000 wounded by the end of the Korean Conflict. Why the huge losses? Because after World War II we were enjoying a "peace dividend" and, feeling secure, we drastically cut our defense budget once again.

Even though the pages of the history books repeatedly show us the danger of gutting our national defense, we seem to be diving back into the dangerous sea of unreadiness like lemmings, unable to help ourselves. Earlier this month — at the same time that North Korea was engaging in a dangerous game of nuclear brinkmanship, and instability was growing in the former Soviet Union, in Africa and in Haiti — the House Armed Services Committee debated and passed a defense bill that was based on budget requests from an administration which seems bent on ignoring the lessons of history.

Although the bill preserved some important programs, it cut others to dangerously low levels, risking readiness and raising the specter of an ill-equipped, poorly trained military. The administration said this year's request would provide $3 billion more in budget authority than last year's bill. After accounting for inflation, however, it was actually $2.5 billion less, and the House cut another $900 million from the request. Real defense spending has undergone a 33.7 percent decrease since fiscal year 1985. Under the current plan, by 1999 that figure will be 40 percent, with a corresponding 30 percent decrease in force levels.

Instant communications and advanced technology which have been developed in recent years have made it crucial for us to have sufficient forces who are ready to mobilize at a moment's notice. Yet the 1995 defense budget cuts more than 180,000 active, reserve and civilian defense personnel — 15,000 every month.

We have also lost the luxury of time where our defense industrial base is concerned, so it is important that we maintain industry that can meet defense needs immediately in the event of a crisis. Yet our defense industrial base is eroding at a record rate. By 1999, employment in the defense sector will be down some 2 million jobs from 1989 levels.

In September 1993, the Clinton administration announced the results of the Bottom Up Review (BUR), calling for the U.S. to downsize its military while still maintaining the capability of dealing with two nearly simultaneous major regional conflicts. However, the BUR reduces military end-strengths across all services except the Marine Corps, and there is serious concern that our forces may be inadequate to execute two concurrent major operations with the forces recommended by the BUR.

In addition, the administration's own estimate under the BUR shows that at least $20 billion in currently unbudgeted defense spending will be required over the next five years just to provide the force structure specified by the BUR. In fact, service leaders have testified before Congress that they cannot fund all of the programs identified under the BUR.

When the administration's own blueprint for downsizing casts doubts upon our ability to meet the challenges of the future, it is time to rethink that blueprint. Current defense policy is a runaway train headed for disaster, and it is time to put on the brakes. We must ensure that our borders are safe, our interests protected abroad and our fighting men and women given the training, support and equipment they need to get the job done.

Cynthia McKinney

Cynthia Ann McKinney was elected Georgia's first African-American congresswoman in November 1992 with 75 percent of the vote. She is the only woman serving in Georgia's congressional delegation.

Congresswoman McKinney serves as a member of the Agriculture Committee and the International Relations Committee. In addition to her committee work, McKinney is an active member of the Congressional Black Caucus, the Women's Caucus and the Progressive Caucus, and served as secretary for the record-breaking freshman class of the 103rd Congress. She was also chosen to head the Women's Caucus Task Force on Children, Youth and Families, the first freshman representative to do so.

From 1988 until 1992, McKinney served in the Georgia House of Representatives, where she worked on civil rights issues, including economic opportunities for minority- and women-owned businesses, and issues related to environmental justice. McKinney gained prominence fighting for fair reapportionment in Georgia.

In 1984, McKinney worked as a diplomatic fellow at Spelman College in Atlanta. She also taught political science at Clark Atlanta University and most recently at Agnes Scott College in Georgia. McKinney served on the board of the HIV Health Services Planning Council of Metro Atlanta and she is a member of the National Council of Negro Women, the NAACP and the Sierra Club.

McKinney received her undergraduate degree in international relations from the University of Southern California in 1978. Currently she is a Ph.D. candidate in international relations at Tufts University's Fletcher School of Law and Diplomacy.

Cynthia McKinney

U.S. House of Representatives
Democrat, Georgia

Cynthia McKinney

[Statement delivered for the introduction of Code of Conduct on Arms Transfers, Washington, D.C., November 18, 1993.]

Mr. Speaker:

As a member of the Georgia State Legislature I gave a controversial speech on the involvement of the United States in the Gulf War. I believed then, as I believe now, that American soldiers should not be victims of a short-sighted foreign policy that provides American support for corrupt and anti-democratic regimes.

That was Cold War thinking — the support of dictators, so long as they were friendly to the U.S. and unfriendly to the Soviet Union. Well, the Soviet Union no longer exists. It is time to end the Cold War thinking that has influenced so much of our policy on arms transfers.

The Children's Defense Fund has a wonderfully provocative poster that reads: "Last year we gave $8 billion in military aid to countries our undereducated children can't even find on a map..."

For the third year in a row, the U.S. retains the world championship in the arms dealing competition. Not only are we the No. 1 arms dealer in the world, but our sales exceed all other competitors combined.

Since the end of World War II, 40 million people have died in wars fought with conventional weapons.

Does selling these weapons make the world a safer place?

Do military aid and arms sales promote stability and economic progress in the developing world?

The Arms Control and Disarmament Agency estimates that each year about $1 trillion is spent on armed forces around the world. A staggering $200 billion of this is spent by developing countries, which is equal to about four times all the bilateral and multilateral foreign assistance they receive.

The arms race taking place in the Third World drains badly needed funds from infrastructure development, social spending, and business investment. Regional competitors strive to keep parity with one another. Sadly, the weapons are as likely to be turned on domestic populations as historic regional enemies.

We simply cannot afford the arms sale frenzy in which we have been engaged. Our children cannot afford it. The children of the developing world cannot afford it.

For years we sold weapons to dictators and provided military training for their officers. We armed the shah of Iran, we armed Iraq, we armed Panama, we armed Somalia and we armed Haiti. We continue to pay for these sales with American tax dollars and American lives.

There are presently some restraints on the arms trade. But the failures of the present regimes are all too apparent. In Haiti, the military that overturned the elected government of President Aristide and scorned the Governors Island accord was comprised of an officer corps trained in America.

At the very least, American arms should not be sold and U.S. military training should not be provided to governments that oppose American principles.

The United States has led the effort to establish the United Nations Register of Conventional Arms and this is an important achievement. The United States has engaged in negotiations to reduce the arms trade in volatile regions of the world. The Foreign Affairs Committee, on which I serve, has eliminated many of the earmarks for military aid and reduced security assistance to countries that abuse human rights. These are important actions.

Despite these efforts, the arms trade continues at an alarming level. Something more is needed to reduce the global trade in conventional arms.

The legislation I introduce today will establish a "code of conduct" for arms sales and transfers. An identical bill is being introduced by my Senate colleague, Senator Mark Hatfield. I believe that this is a sensible approach that will increase the chances that we will at least think about what we are doing — to ourselves, to our children, to the world.

Essentially, the legislation would prohibit United States military assistance and arms transfers to foreign governments that are undemocratic, do not adequately protect human rights, are engaged in acts of armed aggression, or are not fully participating in the United Nations Register of Conventional Arms, unless the Congress acted to approve such a sale or transfer.

Change is always difficult. There are many interests that view arms as export products. I believe we must export products that reflect the American ideal of prosperity and the good life all our neighbors wish to share.

A tremendous grassroots effort is already under way, and I am pleased to include in the Record a listing of religious, international development, human rights, and economic conversion groups who have endorsed the Code of Conduct campaign. I thank them for all their efforts, which have been crucial to the development of this legislation. The work of these citizen groups represents the best of our vital democracy.

We must end the U.S. role in promoting the global arms trade. Otherwise, we will not be able to accomplish the most important jobs ahead of us — investing in our children's health and education, making sure we all have jobs and homes, making sure we have a global economy that is growing and producing markets for American products — and that every country on the map will be one that every child in America can identify.

I urge my colleagues to lend their names to this important effort.

[Editors' notes: Representative McKinney's proposed amendment to the foreign aid bill to block U.S. arms transfers to authoritarian regimes and abusers of human rights was defeated 17 to 18 in the House International Relations Committee in May 1995.

On June 29, 1995, the U.S. Supreme Court ruled McKinney's 11th congressional district in Georgia unconstitutional and left it to the federal courts or state Legislature to draw a new congressional map that does not rely upon race. At publication, the Georgia Legislature was stalemated over redrawing the state's congressional districts.]

Elizabeth Dole

As president of the American Red Cross, Elizabeth Dole continues a remarkable public service career in which she has served six United States presidents and has been named by the Gallup Poll as one of the world's 10 most admired women. In September, 1995, she was named to the National Women's Hall of Fame in Seneca Falls, New York.

A native of Salisbury, North Carolina, Dole graduated with distinction and as a member of Phi Beta Kappa from Duke University. She received her law degree from Harvard Law School and also holds a master's degree in education and government from Harvard.

In February 1983, Dole joined President Reagan's Cabinet as secretary of the U.S. Department of Transportation — the first woman to hold that position. During Dole's four and a half years at Transportation, the United States enjoyed the safest years in its history in all three major transportation areas — rail, air and highway.

Dole was sworn in by President Bush as the nation's 20th secretary of Labor in January 1989. As Labor secretary, Dole served as the president's chief advisor on labor and work force issues. Numerous initiatives to benefit at-risk youth became her top priority — a priority she has pursued at the American Red Cross in establishing the Hanford Foundation in honor of her mother, Mary Hanford.

Dole oversees nearly 30,000 American Red Cross staff members and more than 1.5 million volunteers who comprise the world's foremost humanitarian organization. Dole worked as a member of that volunteer force in 1991, taking no salary her first year as president.

The American Red Cross provides half of America's blood supply. While blood is "overwhelmingly safe," according to the Food and Drug Administration, Dole secured approval of the Board of Governors of the American Red Cross to launch a sweeping $148 million state-of-the-art blood system to quickly and efficiently incorporate medical technology as it evolves. In 1994, Dole received the Maxwell Finland Award from the National Foundation for Infectious Diseases for her efforts.

Responding to more than four years of record-breaking natural disasters, Dole has led aggressive fund-raising efforts resulting in $353 million to assist victims of Hurricane Andrew and Iniki, the Midwest floods, and the California earthquake. Dole has initiated a number of steps to increase financial accountability in the Red Cross. Currently, 93 cents of every dollar contributed goes directly to programs and services.

Dole visited the Persian Gulf following the Gulf War to assess services the Red Cross provided to our armed forces. In December 1992, she visited Red Cross relief facilities in famine-stricken Somalia, Mozambique and war-torn Croatia. More recently, Dole led a humanitarian relief delegation to Rwandan refugee camps.

Elizabeth Dole

President, American Red Cross

Elizabeth Dole

[Speech delivered at Radcliffe College Commencement,
Cambridge, Massachusetts, June 11, 1993.]

Thirty-five years ago this fall, this Dixie native found a second home right here in the heart of Yankee country. My time in Cambridge was a wonderful springboard to public life, for it was here that my curiosity about a career in government and public service became a calling.

I have been asked to share some thoughts this afternoon on women in public policy — an interesting topic, because while there are more women in public leadership roles than in private, there are still relatively few. While there are great opportunities for women in government, there obviously remain impediments.

President Linda Wilson, in proposing Radcliffe's agenda for the 1990s, has said that this institution should be committed to promoting women's participation in shaping public policy. "Women," she said, "...have not had a strong public voice, and they are relatively absent from policymaking roles in general." Unfortunately, she's right about the level of participation and, thanks goodness, she's in exactly the right place to make a difference.

Let me commend you, President Wilson, on your inspired ideas for programs relating to women and public policy like the Distinguished Visitor in Public Policy program, which welcomed Governor Madeleine Kunin as its first participant. President Wilson's leadership inspired the Dean's Office to organize the Radcliffe partnerships allowing students to work closely with influential women — the Bunting Institute Fellows at Radcliffe and the Nieman Fellows at Harvard. As these programs demonstrate, there are many ways to pursue the goal of involving women in shaping public policy.

And there are many reasons to pursue this goal. In the first place, it's right. Too many of our number have felt the sting of discrimination. Secondly, women, I believe, have something very special to offer. As President Wilson said, "Women, as new entrants to the fields, bring fresh ideas, new and different perspectives, new energies and new skills." And thirdly, our work force is changing — as I continually preached at the Labor Department. America must be able to welcome women and minorities into its leadership roles if we are to accommodate that change. Sixty-four percent of the new entrants to the work force over the next 10 years will be women. If the public sector is to attract the best and the brightest, it must be able to attract and reward women.

When I was in law school at Harvard, only 24 of the 550 students were women. There were only a few women, at the time, who had made partner in major American law firms. The private sector simply was not a strong option. Public policy beckoned as a rewarding alternative — a call to service, a chance to make a positive difference in people's lives. I answered the call, and have thanked heaven many times since that I did.

For during those days I walked these grounds — between ski trips to Cannon Mountain and dates in Boston's Back Bay — I managed to make a life-shaping decision that has provided enormous personal satisfaction. I would highly recommend such a choice — a life of public service — to women facing similar decisions today, and for similar reasons.

There are, however, some observations I could offer to the Radcliffe student of 1993 which might smooth the way a little. And I could summarize them this way: that our greatest obstacle — that we are women in a world of men — is really an enormous opportunity, if we will just see it that way.

Remember the question Henry Higgins asked in the film *My Fair Lady*, "Why can't a woman be more like a man?" Why can't a woman be more like a man? That's the question Susan B. Anthony asked America in 1873, insisting that women have the right to vote. "How can the consent of the governed be given, if the right to vote is denied?" she asked.

Why can't a woman be more like a man? That was the question I pondered while here at school, surveying the choices men had when leaving this leafy, academic village. Others were obviously asking this question as well. I am reminded of the day here in Cambridge when my unoccupied car rolled down a driveway and slammed into another car. In the course of cleaning up the wreck, I became friends with its owner — Pat Schroeder. Pat also followed a calling into public service, and is today an influential congresswoman from Colorado.

In fact, today there is a lot more opportunity than impediment in public service. When the United States Senate convened this January, there were six women senators — triple the number of the previous all-time high. And when it meets next week, there will be seven, as Kay Bailey Hutchison takes the oath of office on Monday. On the other side of the Capitol dome, 47 women were sworn into the House of Representatives — a gain of 19 from the previous Congress, another all-time high. At the state level, women now hold 22.2 percent of state offices — you guessed it, another all-time high. And, perhaps most encouragingly, women continue to make dramatic gains in state legislatures — which often serve as a pipeline to higher office. In 1971, 4.7 percent of state legislators were women. Today that number is 20.2 percent.

I think it's important, however, to learn the correct lesson from our successes. Further gains do not depend on better answers to the question, "Why can't a woman be more like a man?" The question we should be asking now is, "Why can't a woman be more like a woman?"

I'd like to quote for you from a recent article in *Life* magazine: *Women, the article asserts, are more committed than men to cushioning the hard corners of the country, to making it simply a safer place. Women want stricter law enforcement against drunk driving and illegal firearms and drug dealing... It's not that men don't care about these issues. It's simply that women care more.*

I don't know if that's true. But perhaps our approach is different. Perhaps our involvement in public policy debates provides a leavening influence. Perhaps more women in public service would result in greater focus on cushioning corners for vulnerable Americans. If that's so, then it's doubly important that we women add our voices to the national debates, that we take our places at the tables of power, that we rise to the challenge of leadership when we believe that to be our calling. And, as it turns out, we may be very well-suited for that calling.

A new trend is "female-style management." Soft is hard, according to Tom Peters, the renowned management guru who has spent more than a decade in search of excellence. What that means is probably best explained by the woman president of Tenneco's natural gas subsidiary, an industry traditionally dominated by "good old boys." Rebecca McDonald says, *You hear a lot of talk about changing the way we teach little girls because they are taught to listen and accommodate, while little boys are taught to win at all costs. I wonder if, really, we shouldn't rethink the way we're teaching boys. The rigidity that comes from expecting to win at all costs doesn't necessarily play to the new skill sets we need to manage and lead today.*

The management skills she refers to include mediation, negotiation, and dealing with needs, issues and forces that are often not clearly defined. And, as McDonald points out, *Women have a higher tolerance for ambiguity because we're always responsible for tending to the emotional needs of others, which are very fluid. We learn to read between the lines and come up with creative solutions for accommodating people.* So then, why can't a woman be more like a woman? In other words, to some extent progress for women in public policy and private life may indeed hinge on our ability to acknowledge and develop our skills and values as women. It may just be that those are the skills and values our country needs most at this moment.

I have been privileged during my years in public service to work with a number of successful women in public policy and I would like to pass along some of their observations, and some of my own, about drawing on our professional, female advantages.

The first is to take full advantage of our trumpeted trait of flexibility — in fact, to plan for the unexpected, and relish our ability to think on our feet.

I'll tell you a story from the salad days of my career to illustrate the point. I had taken a month off between jobs to learn my way around the courtroom, observing proceedings in the Washington, D.C., night court. On my third night there, as I was sitting in the front row, the judge asked me what I was doing there, and whether I was a member of the D.C. Bar. I told him I was Elizabeth Hanford, and I was observing court proceedings so I could learn to take cases for indigents. And yes, I was a member of the Bar. No sooner had I said that than I was handed a file and told I was to defend an indigent. That night. Minutes later I was in a cell block trying to talk to my first client — a Greek national who spoke very little English, and who was charged with petting, and thereby annoying, a lion at the National Zoo. When the proceedings got under way that evening, the opposing counsel was a Harvard classmate of mine — No. 1 in my class — Lee Freeman, editor of the *Harvard Law Review*. I argued that, without the lion as a witness, there was no way of knowing whether or not he had been "annoyed or teased." By the grace of God, I won the case.

Rigid guidelines, set agendas and line-reporting responsibilities all help create the illusion of control in the current management environment. But perhaps a knack for flexibility is more important. As Madeleine Kunin has said, women need to value their own experiences more, and recognize the skills they have taken from them. *Anyone who's been in a volunteer organization or done things in the community, is superbly equipped for political life,* she said. *You have your finger on the pulse of the community that way, and you learn to be an organizer... Most women have learned to organize their lives because they've had to juggle so much.*

I can't help but add to what Madeleine said, since planning for the unexpected is the day-to-day work of the Red Cross. We don't know when or where the next tornado or flood will hit. We don't know when or where someone will need blood, but we do know we'll be called to help, and we are confident we can respond. We plan for what we cannot predict.

Another observation I have is that to succeed in the public arena women must learn to trust their instincts. It's not just female intuition — it's a cognitive skill that we are perhaps more open to. Estimation skills are now being taught to children as they come up through elementary and secondary schools, and instinct is often another word for it. It's an ability to take in a great deal of information and quickly reduce it to a rough, but generally accurate picture. It's the soft route to hard data.

Yet too often we women allow ourselves to be intimidated into denying our instincts — whether it's a judgment of people, situations or the heart of a policy question. The women in this audience have probably all had the experience of sitting across the table from someone — a man, let's say — with whom you disagree. Ask yourselves: how many times, in this situation, has your reaction been to question your own judgment rather than his — only to find out later that you were right on the money?

Over the ages, we women have perfected to a high art form this trait of second-guessing ourselves. Perhaps it stems from our early and constant exposure to society's message that female traits and talents are inferior, but we have to get over it. It takes confidence to trust ourselves, and if we don't have confidence, our voices will be lost if ever they're heard.

My third observation is that our personal integrity — our moral compass — counts far more than any line on a resume. Barbara Jordan, Nancy Kassebaum and Margaret Thatcher are three who've succeeded in the world of public policy and politics. And agree with their positions or not, one of the hallmarks of their service is their total and complete commitment to integrity. In a world where we are constantly dealing with problems that other people create for us, integrity is one area over which each of us has 100 percent control. Without that personal set of values, it's impossible to make consistent decisions or to inspire confidence and trust.

It's interesting to note that the American Management Association surveyed 1,500 managers around the country and asked the open-ended question, "What values, personal traits or characteristics do you look for and admire in your superiors?" More than 225 different responses emerged, but the most frequent response — ranked No. 1 by 83 percent of the managers — was integrity. Opinion polls tell us that women are viewed by most of the public as generally more trustworthy than men. I'm not sure that perception is accurate. But it does present an opportunity for women to lead, and with it comes a responsibility to live up to the public trust. In a world taken over by cynicism and mistrust of our institutions, women can offer hope.

That was on my mind when I became president of the American Red Cross two years ago. The spotlight of public scrutiny has been shining harshly on nonprofit institutions of late. Whether it's been charities or universities in the news, often the news hasn't been good. Everything from academic policies to accounting practices to relief services has become the focus of national debate, fodder for critical headlines and footage for *Sixty Minutes* exposes. The public trust has been shaken.

I assembled our headquarters staff and told them that I considered our most important mission to be the renewal of the trust historically associated with the patches on our sleeves, and the flags in the field. We are the creation of a benevolent society whose people use us to reinforce their values and to achieve their higher goals, and we must live up to our trust. Now is not the time to shrink from scrutiny. We, and other members of the nonprofit sector, must welcome it, open ourselves to it. And in doing so, we must open ourselves to change, acknowledge error where we have erred and accept some direction from those we serve. Charities, universities, and other nonprofits are being held responsible in ways they never have before, and we must recognize this as a good thing. Individuals and institutions who succeed in this new, more media-intense world will be those who are willing to listen to — and respond to — a much more sophisticated and demanding public.

The fourth common denominator I have seen among successful women leaders is a commitment to those who follow. Radcliffe is a co-sponsor of the Women's Leadership Conference, an example of just that kind of commitment. It was organized by undergraduates who are concerned that while women constitute at least 40 percent of the undergraduate population, they represent only a very small percentage of the student leadership. About 20 years ago, a group of us formed an organization called "Executive Women in Government," which still flourishes today. Its purpose is twofold: to help younger women who want to follow into public service by giving them information and advice, and to make it easier for women in policymaking positions to relate to one another across government. Networking — women reaching out to other women — is a way of using our special opportunities to overcome obstacles. I have been helped many times in many stages of my career by women who were ahead of me. As a result, my door is always open to young women who are in need of a mentor, and I would encourage other women to do the same.

The fifth and final challenge for women is not to let others define success for us. It's a tempting trap, but an unfulfilling one. If we are to grow and succeed, then we cannot let others dictate what is right for us. Neither our friends nor our colleagues — male or female — can make the tough decisions for us.

In the summer of 1987, I grappled with a decision affecting my career. I was secretary of Transportation, and wanted to resign to campaign for my husband, who was seeking the presidency of the United States. A lot of people didn't understand. Why should I have to quit my job, they asked, to play the role of "good wife"? While the people asking the question probably considered themselves quite "liberated," what they were really asking was, "Why can't a woman be more like a man?" My decision was to take time out to support my husband. It was an exhilarating and challenging learning experience, and a chance to participate in the high point, to date, of my husband's career. I made that choice not because I had to, but because I wanted to. Taking that step was important to my personal fulfillment.

I'm sure every women in this audience has been forced to make difficult choices like mine. Our lives are complicated with balancing personal and professional goals, loving our families while searching for individual fulfillment. And every woman must find her own answers, answers that are right for her. We must not move from one inhibiting dogma to another, from insisting women stay at home to making them feel guilty if they do. We women must allow ourselves, and each other, the freedom to choose.

My mother has always been a strong, wise force in my life — a reckoning star as I've charted my course. She has often been uncertain about some of my life steps — like deciding to go to law school — but she has concentrated her advice on the values behind the decisions. Two years ago the power mavens in Washington also questioned why I would resign from the Cabinet again, this time to head up a charity, of all things — even if it was the largest humanitarian organization in America. My mother reminded me that she had once served as a Red Cross volunteer during World War II. And she said, "Elizabeth, nothing I ever did made me feel so important." Women across America are discovering that feeling in as many ways as there are women — some through public service, some in the world of business or as lawyers and doctors, and some as wives, mothers and volunteers. No one can or should tell us where we will find that feeling, or how we will come to define our own success. Those are decisions we alone can make for ourselves.

In the fairy tales we were read as children, once having been rescued by the prince, the "female lead" lives happily ever after. That was the theme of *Cinderella*, *Snow White* and *Sleeping Beauty*. But now perhaps we need to read our daughters a new bedtime story — with a heroine who isn't a princess, but a woman who sees that there are things that need to be changed to make life better for herself and others. A woman who's not a victim, and who doesn't need a rescuer. We need a tale about a woman whose talents and abilities are valued and admired, a woman who uses those talents to succeed, a woman who's committed, who feels passionately about her life's decisions. We need a story to inspire our little girls to be more like themselves. Such a story would not be a fairy tale. The other recipients of the award given this morning are such examples, and there are hundreds of others under this tent here in Radcliffe Yard. And if each of us continues to ask the right question, "Why can't a woman be more like a woman?" there will be hundreds of thousands more tomorrow.

Thank you very much, and thank you, again, for the great honor of receiving the Radcliffe Medal.

Lynn Martin

After serving as the 21st secretary of Labor under President George Bush, Lynn Martin is engaged in a number of activities focused on the future of the United States economy and the American work force.

During her tenure as secretary, she focused the Labor Department on what she believes is a revolution in the workplace. Congressional passage of the administration's proposal for increased pension portability was part of her strategy to give America's working men and women the capability to be secure in today's rapidly changing global economy.

The centerpiece of this strategy was her emphasis on a high-skills, high-paid work force. Under her leadership, the department developed proposals to achieve this goal. These included: Job Training 2000, a national youth apprenticeship system; a nationwide effort to implement the recommendations of the Secretary's Commission on Achieving Necessary Skills; pension opportunities for workers' expanded retirement; the "Glass Ceiling" Initiative, and a reorganization of the department to create a renewed agency focused on the new American workplace.

Martin also focused on programs to assist displaced homemakers and open opportunities for women in nontraditional jobs. As secretary, Martin put forth a model workplace program at the Department of Labor, believing that the government should lead by example. Department employees received sexual harassment training and diversity training. The department also underwent its own glass ceiling review. In a unique effort to move beyond the confines of her office and to keep in close touch with people working in different jobs, Martin regularly spent time working at jobs ranging from department store clerk, to pipe welding, to making French fries at McDonald's.

Prior to serving as secretary of Labor, Martin, a Chicago native, represented an Illinois district in the U.S. House of Representatives from 1981 to 1991. During her service in the House, she was the first woman to achieve an elective leadership post when, in 1984, her colleagues chose her to be vice chair of the House Republican Conference, a position she held for four years. Martin served on the House Rules Committee, the House Armed Services Committee, the House Budget Committee (where for a time she was the ranking Republican), the Committee on Public Works and Transportation, and the Committee on the District of Columbia.

Martin now chairs Deloitte & Touche's Council on the Advancement of Women and is an advisor to the firm. She is a regular panelist on public television's *To the Contrary*. She also appears as a frequent guest commentator on the economy on national television and writes opinion columns for national publications. Martin regularly addresses America's businesses and universities on the changing global economic and political environment. She serves on numerous boards of private and public businesses, and has assumed the Davee chair at the J.L. Kellogg Graduate School of Management at Northwestern University.

Lynn Martin

U.S. Secretary of Labor
(1991-1993)

Lynn Martin

[Statement delivered at Washington, D.C., Press Conference, March 24, 1995.]

During the past few weeks, I have received countless offers of help and contributions from friends, allies and, very surprising to me, from people I have never met.

It is for them that a decision about running for the highest elective office in the country, running to try to be president of the United States, had to be made.

First, I ask you to understand what an extraordinary statement that is for me to make — even to come to the belief that one could be any kind of president. It is mind boggling for someone born in 1939, and for a woman who was clueless about her future when she graduated from college in 1960.

To go beyond that and seriously consider a presidential run for the only real reason one should run — because you think you could be the best person for the men and women and children of this nation — represents the kind of self-confidence that is very difficult for someone who ran for eighth-grade president and lost by one vote, her own, to project. But considering a run for the presidency is exactly what I've been doing.

I found out that I wanted to run for president, and I believe that, at least most of the time, I would bring the kind of intelligence, integrity and strength the job needs. I also would bring to the presidency a belief in individuals, a willingness to provoke discussion, and a clear-headed idea of where this nation needs to go and how to get us there.

But to be president, you have to run. There's no gender preference here. There's no extra boost that might help for those who have been precluded from some experiences that make it easier.

So, like every presidential candidate, I examined my personal and professional resources, the time and commitment required, the possibility of winning and losing, the effects on my family and found that those were all just excuses for the real question. One cannot be Hamlet perusing the universe while the world passes one by. I cannot and will not lay my decision on any member of my family.

My husband, who is a federal judge, couldn't be involved in the campaign and would probably be glad of that. My sister only asked that I tell her if I was going to run so she wouldn't be the last to know. The children, my two daughters and my five stepchildren, are a bit bemused by this whole process and, bluntly, none of them are the type to look adoringly at me while I make some purportedly brilliant comment. But they would all help and support me. My decision has little to do with spending more time with them. Although I do not give up my right to make them feel guilty in countless other ways, this time they are free.

No, this decision is mine. And my decision is that I will not run for the Republican nomination for president of the United States. I would not bring the full commitment of time, energy, and person that the next year requires and that the run deserves. In other words, although I finally may have found out I really could be president, I cannot convince myself I would progress along in the campaign as one must.

Groucho Marx once joked, in a bittersweet way, after a country club that refused him membership initially changed its tune when it needed something from him, "I don't choose to join any country club that would have me as a member." Although it's not a perfect analogy, there's some comparison.

This, my decision not to run, has little to do with the issue of abortion. Certainly being pro-choice did not deter me. A good candidate convinces people on many issues. It's not even about today's campaign tactics, although some of them are certainly despicable. It's not even about the media. I stole a dollar from my mother's drawer when I was five, bought candy and promptly threw up for two days. I suspect I'd have the same reaction when you discovered I wasn't perfect. But you go on.

No, the decision is recognizing I am unwilling to put forward what the public rightfully demands of its candidates — an uncomplaining, committed person who puts her or his time, reputation and life totally on the line. My only regret is that this means it is unlikely that any woman will compete for the top spot on either the Republican or Democratic ticket in 1996. A smaller talent pool is never a good idea to get the best people.

The current candidates have ideas and a passion about the future. A few of them could be very good presidents. Maybe one of them will put his idea of the best person for the vice president on the ballot and she will do a great job.

I don't "do" nobility well. It does not matter if I'm on the ticket or even in the race. What does matter is that in this country, unlike far too many others, men and women know they have a chance to be the best. As we move toward the next century, that goal is getting closer.

For myself, I will continue to speak out for those ideas and ideals that will help my party and this nation steer a better course toward the future.

I believe when we talk about welfare reform we must also look at a program that treats pregnant girls under the age of 15 who keep their babies in a far different way than we treat a 30-year-old having her fifth child.

I believe the future for small and medium-sized businesses should be our focus. These folks are tomorrow's economy — women, men, minorities — companies without vice presidents of government affairs — companies who are the pioneers on a new kind of technological soil.

I believe we must talk about the specifics of eliminating our deficit; boring, mundane, and absolutely necessary for the next generation.

I believe we must have a foreign policy that recognizes the United States as the greatest power in the world, not a craven sycophant at the tables of lesser nations.

And I believe in the idea and the ideal that no one — not the young African-American male in South-Central Los Angeles, nor the mother of three in Appalachia, nor the recent immigrant in South Florida — no one is etched forever in one spot in this society, and is without the essential dignity that surpasses anything that the state can have.

So, I'm incredibly pleased that so many people urged me to make the race; that they believed in me. Any disappointment I have caused with this announcement is sincerely appreciated. This announcement, after all, is not an obituary.

Madeleine May Kunin

There was little doubt, after President Bill Clinton was elected, that former Governor Madeleine Kunin of Vermont would have a prominent place in the new administration. As the first woman governor of that state, and only the third Democrat, Kunin distinguished herself in her three terms as a dynamic, reform-minded presence in the political world who achieved significant reform in the areas of education, the environment, and children's services.

During Governor Kunin's tenure in office, teacher salaries in Vermont moved from the rank of 49th in the nation to 26th, access to kindergarten was guaranteed, and early childhood programs were expanded. She also achieved significant advances in school finance reform, business-education partnerships, and vocational education reform. *Fortune* magazine listed Kunin as one of the 10 best education governors in the nation. Vermont was cited by the Institute for Southern Studies as the No. 1 state for its environmental policies, children's services and care of the mentally ill.

Bill Clinton chose Kunin as one of three members of his vice-presidential search committee. She was appointed deputy secretary of the U.S. Department of Education in January 1993, and has worked closely with Secretary Richard Riley and the administration on key issues of education reform. These include the Goals 2000 Act, the School-to-Work Opportunities Act, the National Service Program, and the Safe and Drug-Free Schools Act. She is co-chair of the Clinton administration's working group on violence prevention.

The deputy secretary has played a leading role in the administration's innovative student loan reform initiative, and the direct lending program, which is expected to save the nation's taxpayers $4 billion in the first five years. She has been the official in charge of the restructuring of the Department of Education's management policies.

Kunin's experience in politics is extensive. Prior to becoming governor, she served three terms in the Vermont General Assembly, where she was elected assistant Democratic Party leader and chaired the Appropriations Committee. She served two terms as lieutenant governor. She is the only woman in the nation to have served three terms as governor, and she continues to be a leading national voice on issues involving reform and equal rights for women.

Born in Zurich, Switzerland, Kunin emigrated to the United States in 1940. She is the author of a memoir, *Living a Political Life*, published by Alfred A. Knopf in 1994.

Madeleine May Kunin

U.S. Deputy Secretary of Education

Madeleine May Kunin

[These remarks are reprinted with permission from *The Commonwealth*, based on a speech delivered in San Francisco before the Commonwealth Club of California, October 28, 1994.]

I cannot tell you that everything is perfect in the American classroom; I wish that I could. But by the same token, reports implying that public education is on its last legs and should be put out of its misery are false. We have some terrific schools in this country — schools that you would be thrilled to have your child attend — where there is learning and discipline and laughter. But we also have schools that don't succeed, where the paint is peeling, the hallways are dangerous — and the bathrooms more so — and faith in the children's ability to learn has crumbled under the weight of poverty and exhaustion.

We are poised today at a critical juncture in education. Do we build on the schools that we know work, or do we cave in to the naysayers, who tell us public education can't work? As you might suspect, I am an optimist, and the reasons I am are twofold. If we can have excellent schools in one neighborhood, they why can't we have them in the one nearby?

Our problem isn't that we don't know what is needed to provide our children with an excellent education in a safe setting, because we do. Models of success exist at Central Park East Middle School in Harlem; Hope High School in Providence, Rhode Island; Wheeler Elementary School in Louisville, Kentucky, and right here, in California. These tell us that if we have high expectations, then children win in performance, and if we have families involved, then we get extraordinary results.

My second reason for optimism is that, for the first time, we have the tools at hand to duplicate, replicate, and imitate success on a grand scale. President Clinton, Secretary Riley, and a broad coalition of education boosters — including the business community — enabled us to win passage of every piece of legislation proposed to the Congress, the last of which, the reauthorized Elementary and Secondary Education Act (ESEA), was signed by the president last week. This was truly a remarkable record in these contentious times. What are the central themes of these new laws: the Goals 2000 Act, the School-to-Work Opportunities Act, and the new ESEA? The themes are higher standards and the belief that every child can learn.

For the first time, we have a set of national goals, set in law and agreed upon by an overwhelming majority of Americans, that include investment in professional development for teachers, the necessity for safe and disciplined schools, and the importance of family involvement in children's success. I would add, although you won't see it in the law, there is optimism and the belief that every child can learn more, do better, and that our school system can, in fact, be improved.

Why were we, and therefore you, the American people, successful in the Congress? Strong bipartisan support, a broad coalition — the president, the Congress, the nation's governors, unions, school board members, superintendents, parents — all joined hands and never let go in support of this package. We were able to avoid polarization on hot-button issues, like school prayer and sex education, and stick to the basics, like improving teaching and learning.

This is a remarkable coalition which never existed before, and for the first time we have not only the legislation, but the demonstrated community support to improve the schools of America on a large scale. This same coalition is already forming in many states and communities, and therein lies our hope. But it will take more than new laws, technical assistance, dynamic partnerships, and even a modest amount of new funding to keep the promise so fundamental to democracy: that you can be anything you want to be in this country, if you work hard and get a good education. It will be the belief that every child can learn.

This is a simple statement, but one that has received more good intentions than real action.

For a great many years, the underlying philosophy that has guided so much of American education is that some children are smarter, some will just muddle through, and some children are incapable of learning. We accepted the unstated assumption that the poor and disadvantaged could only master a watered-down curriculum, and so that was what we gave them, assuming we were being kind. But we were not. Low expectations, of course, are always met.

Our attention and commitment to excellence at every level of American education is something very new, refreshing, and long overdue, because we know that in this democracy and this economy, no one can be wasted and left for years to flounder, unemployed and uneducated. This optimistic message stands in sharp contrast to the current intellectual inquiry-making. *The Bell Curve* may be a best-seller, but it throws a curve at the very mission of American education. It says, in essence, that education, hard work, and tenacity do not matter.

There is some good news in education. We have growing evidence that hard work and tough courses continue to pay off. For example, black students who take calculus in high school, as opposed to only algebra, score 100 points more on the SAT math test. A similar result is found on the math skills section of the National Assessment of Education Progress. African-American 17-year-olds with pre-calculus or calculus, compared to those with only algebra or general math, scored 60 points higher. Our message says that every child can have his or her mind grow with the excitement and discipline of learning.

We have moved from the politics of blame — blaming teachers, parents, and even students themselves — to the politics of results, concentrating on concrete and practical results driven by high standards. We have moved from concentrating, not on what pulls us apart, but on what brings us together. A key player in this transition to positive results has been the business community. You are excellent translators, putting into concrete terms why educational excellence is so important. You know what is at stake. Each person deprived of an education is deprived of employment and a decent life, and in the end, our country will be deprived of its foundation of equal opportunity for all.

Happily, we have a model of success right here at J. Haley Durham Elementary School in Fremont, California, which has just been designated one of America's Blue Ribbon Schools at a recent White House ceremony. The students who go to Durham, unlike the majority of Fremont students, are not middle class. Fifty-three percent of the students receive free or reduced-cost lunches. Nearly one in five come from families on welfare, and about half of the students qualify for our Chapter 1 program for disadvantaged children. Here is a picture of a school that seems to have the deck stacked against it, and for many years the students at Durham did not achieve. The school's curricula were defined by three Rs: remediation, retention, and repetition. Today, everything is different; Durham is an achieving and exciting place to learn.

My point here is simple, but fundamental. Eleven years after the report *A Nation at Risk* told us that our schools were becoming mediocre, we are putting the pieces together, turning the corner, building partnerships, and bringing reform to scale. American education has standards to improve, and there is a story here that needs to be told.

Here a comment on Proposition 187 [a ballot initiative, approved by California voters November 8, 1994, to deny public education to undocumented immigrant children] is in order. America's schools are terribly burdened by many of the social problems of our society. If we have a problem, we tell our schools to fix the problem, be it gang violence, teenage pregnancy, or illegal aliens. The result is that our schools are increasingly losing their focus on academics. The school day is being picked apart, so that just over 40 percent of the day is spent on core academics. This is the national average. That is much too low, particularly when compared to our European neighbors, who spend twice the time on academic subjects. I am concerned that asking teachers and administrators to become part-time employees of the Border Patrol will only increase the erosion of the school day and burden teachers with endless paperwork, when they should be teaching. But perhaps most destructive of all, it would pit child against child, parent against parent, and drain schools of their ability to be safe and supportive communities that foster growth and learning.

If we want to prepare our young people for life in the 21st century, we need to keep our focus on teaching and learning. We also want to reaffirm in the strongest way that our young people are not learning as Republicans or Democrats; they are learning as the Americans who are the future of our country. That is why the president's initiatives are important. They are, first, new funding and strengthening of Head Start, to make sure that young children who get ahead, stay ahead. Second is the Safe and Drug-Free Schools Act, which would support safe after-school programs. We want the guns out of the schools. We simply aren't going to tolerate 14-year-olds proving their manhood by threatening the lives of other children. Third is the first real funding for taking technology into schools and reshaping the classrooms of the future. Number four is the fundamental revision of the Elementary and Secondary Education Act to place a new and proper emphasis on high expectations for all children. We want to encourage innovation and flexibility, and schools simply need to have more choices. We want to support and encourage the development of charter schools and schools-within-schools.

Five is Goals 2000, which encourages every school community to find its own way to improve learning without burdensome federal mandates. Six is the National Service Program for 20,000 young Americans, which is already bigger than the Peace Corps at its peak. Seven is a redirection of our research arm. Number eight, and one of the most exciting things, is a School-to-Work initiative that will help to connect many more young people to the world of work. We want to jump-start young people into thinking about their careers by creating demanding apprenticeships that will give them an early focus on life.

Finally, going to college costs more money, and families who have children in college and adults going back to school to build second careers are looking for help. So we have created a new direct-lending program that gives people the opportunity to create a new and flexible repayment schedule. It means that people struggling to make ends meet can know that whether they have finished school, are looking for work, or just starting a career, they have the option, if they choose, to fit their repayment schedule to their financial condition.

We are pleased that we are united and headed in the right direction, but we also know that none of this will really matter unless we reconnect the American family to the process of learning. Any effort to create top-down reform that excludes the hopes and desires of parents is doomed to failure. Every study shows there is a clear linkage between school success and parental involvement. This, you say, is not news. But it is news to a great many people and to many families that have had to put education on automatic pilot, hoping against hope, in the hurry and stress of putting food on the table, that their sons and daughters will get the education they deserve.

The reality is that many parents find it difficult to visit their children's schools, volunteer, or help with homework, because they simply cannot carve out the time from work, especially when both parents are working, or when one is the sole wage-earner. There is a disturbing additional fall-off in parent participation once children enter high school. The result is that even the most simple, common-sense education practices that have been at the core of family and home life are sometimes given second place.

To their credit, many forward-thinking corporations recognize the changing family-work responsibilities and have initiated family policies that can be replicated throughout corporate America. Wells Fargo Bank is a case in point. This corporation offers family medical leave for newborns, time off for PTA meetings, child development seminars for employees, and flex-time scheduling. The bank also maintains a full-time dependent care referral service for children and older family members.

American education is moving forward. We have proven that we have the capacity to improve education. We have many models of success, and now we have the tools to replicate them. We are the most productive nation on earth; that is both a testament to our educational system and proof that we can fix what ails it. What ails it is not that we don't know how to educate some Americans to high standards and contemporary skills.

The good, old-fashioned American Dream was good to each one of you no doubt because of your ability to get an excellent education. It was the education system of this country that enabled me and my mother and brother to arrive on the shores of this country many years ago, not speaking a word of English, and to develop our minds and dream big dreams. My mother believed, without a doubt, that "anything is possible in America." That optimism was her greatest gift to me. That dream must be our gift to this generation of young Americans, whether they are immigrants from other shores or from the fringe of poverty. We believe that we will and must succeed.

Answers to Written Questions from the Floor:

Q. What is your view on bilingual education? How far can we go to provide it, and how much can we afford to spend on it?
A. The point of education in the American school system is for all children to be able to learn in English as soon as possible. The big question is, how do you get there? For some children the road is to be educated in their own language first and then gradually to go into English. In my own case, I was the only child that didn't speak English in my classroom, so I had to use the swim or sink method. The goal is to develop educated citizens without denying the richness they bring with them from their own countries. It takes a long time for a mature country to accept that.

Q. What is the role of the administration in K through 12 education, and how does it complement the roles played by the states and the local school districts?
A. In many ways, the states got started first. They began the reform efforts after the *A Nation at Risk* report was issued. It was the nation's governors who then said, "How do we know we are moving in the right direction? How do we know we are meeting world-class standards?" President Bush called a meeting of the nation's governors, and a little-known governor from Arkansas was there to hammer out the goals. That was the first time we reached a consensus, but it came from the states initially. We still believe that we need some kind of compass to see whether we are moving in the right direction. I know there are some

skeptics that say that "this is a new federal bureaucracy and federal intrusion." That is absolutely not accurate; we are in fact being less intrusive than ever before. With three former governors involved in this, President Clinton, [Education] Secretary [Richard] Riley, and myself, we are very sensitive to federal mandates. We have not forgotten everything we learned in the last 20 years. We also know that it won't work unless there is local engagement, local participation, and local ideas. That has been the strength of our system of education.

Q. How does parental involvement make a difference in the education of my child? What data do you have on success, IQ, or motivation?

A. We have a lot of data, and there is a report that the Department of Education issued recently about strong families and strong schools. There are very simple things that you may take for granted. Read to your child. The correlation between reading, learning to read, learning to write, and learning to speak is enormously powerful. Having reading material in the home is very important. A child imitates what a parent does, and if a parent is reading, then a child will play at reading. There is a correlation between the amount of television children watch and their success in school. And homework does matter; there is a real connection between success and homework. In fact, a study that the Department of Education released some years ago showed that children who are considered to have less ability can do as well in school — if they do homework — as children who are considered to have higher ability. Homework can close the gap, in many cases. This is particularly significant for high school students. At the bottom of all of this is a parent's communication of whether or not he or she thinks education and learning are important. There is a connection between what is valued at home and what is valued in school.

Q. Opponents of Proposition 187 claim that the U.S. Department of Education will cut off federal spending for the state's schools if the measure is implemented. Is this true?

A. It is highly likely that funds will be cut off, because that is what the law requires.

Q. Critics of the public school system cite an entrenched bureaucracy of administrators and teachers who resist reform. What is your view of this criticism?

A. In some instances, this may be accurate; in other instances, it is not. The schools that work best are those in which the teachers are part of the reform and are invited in from the start. It is the same for parents. Parents need to be engaged at the outset. It takes a lot of work to do it with community, parent, teacher, and administrator inclusion. We have to work harder at freeing schools from some of the bureaucracy. Teachers and principals have to fight for what they believe in. We also have to train people to overcome bureaucracies and become exciting innovators and leaders. They need to take responsibility not only for determining what happens in the classroom, but also for what happens in the whole school.

Q. How can we attract and retain the best and brightest of today's college graduates, particularly people of color, to a career in teaching?

A. This is a major concern, because the proportion of African-American educators to African-American students is very small. There are a few things that may help. One is the

National Service, which will enable more young people to do community service. They will be paid $4,750 a year for the service, and then will be able to repay their student loans according to their income. We might have to do more outreach, and we have to make teaching a profession that has less burnout in it. Many idealistic young people find that their preparation for teaching is not related to the reality they face when they enter the classroom. The Department of Education recently held a seminar with teachers and deans of education to try to figure out what teachers should know before they get into teaching. Hopefully, we will encourage a diverse teaching body as well as a diverse student body.

Q. Some studies say that IQ — and not environment, good nutrition, or role models — makes the biggest difference in how much and how fast a child can learn. Are programs such as Head Start, free school breakfasts, and others a waste of money?

A. No, they are not a waste of money. But none of them alone is a total answer. We know that Head Start, if sustained, makes a big difference. We have another program that is a cousin of Head Start called Even Start that works with preschoolers and parents. It teaches parents literacy and provides preschool care for young children. The program is being carefully evaluated by the Department of Education, and it looks very promising. Children enrolled in Even Start do twice as well on their test scores as children in a comparable group who are not enrolled. Interestingly enough, the parents by and large get their GEDs, and they also remain engaged in their children's learning. We have to recognize that there are other factors that affect test scores. More children are living in poverty in this country than ever before. Young children do not often have basic nutrition, immunization, or the stimulus necessary for growth and development. We also know that all of these factors can be remedied. Nobody can say that Head Start has totally changed things, and nobody can say that removing all lead paint has totally changed things. The positive approach is not to present young people with a sense of fatalism that says, "your status is predetermined," but to change their environment to the greatest extent possible and provide hope.

Q. What is the role of community colleges in our educational system? Can they bridge the gap for those who are not going to get a bachelor's degree or higher?

A. Community colleges are playing an increasingly significant role. More and more students, in order to be employable, need to have some education beyond high school. The School-to-Work program fosters these kinds of partnerships by enabling students to make that transition as part of their normal education. Also we need a partnership with the workplace, in which students learn workplace skills and academic skills and the connection between the two. We have a global reputation for excellent higher education, and students from all over the world come to the U.S. to study. But those schools are excellent because they have undergraduates that by and large come from our American education system. There isn't quite as wide a disparity between our K through 12 system and our higher education system. One reason is that the higher education system is still highly selective in relative terms.

Q. How is the student loan program going? What measures have been taken to reduce misuse of funds, non-repayment of loans, and other types of fraud?

A. The student loan program is increasingly important for American students. It is estimated that half of the 20 million students and their families will require some kind of loan or grant, either subsidized or unsubsidized, to pay for continuing education. We have a responsibility in this regard to several groups. One is to the students themselves, to provide access. Number two is to the institutions, so that they can function in an efficient manner; third is to the taxpayers, to make sure they are not ripped off, and that the debt gets repaid. Progress on reduction in loan defaults is good, but it is not where it should be. We reduced the default rate from about 22 percent five years ago to 15 percent today. Being able to repay loans according to income will become more available to more students. This should also help to reduce defaults. A new program is the direct student loan. The Congress enacted that this year, and so far, 5 percent of the loan volume is in the direct loan program, which cuts out the middle man. The federal government is able to save money by providing loans at a lower rate and with reduced fees. We are shortly going to gear up to 40 percent. It is very unusual for a bureaucracy to be told, "We really like what you are doing." That is exactly the kind of message we are getting from the schools. We believe we are on the right track in making colleges more accessible and affordable, and at the same time, making it clear that you have to be responsible.

Q. How can we ensure that girls have equal opportunity for success in the classroom?

A. By and large, there is equality of opportunity for girls and women. One piece of good news is that there are now more women enrolled in college than men. The percentage of women in graduate school is rising rapidly also. Where there is a problem, it is very subtle. Girls sometimes are rewarded for being quiet and sitting with their hands folded in their laps. Boys are rewarded for waving their arms. Our biggest enemy right now is cynicism and skepticism that we can't govern ourselves and that the system doesn't work. The system is only as good as the people who participate in it, and there is great room for idealism. The power of an individual voice that finds an echo with others is still enormous, and the democratic system is alive and well — as long as we don't let it wither by neglect.

Jeane J. Kirkpatrick

After more than four years (1981 - 1985) as the United States ambassador to the United Nations and member of the Cabinet, the first woman to serve in that office, Jeane J. Kirkpatrick, resumed her position as Leavey Professor at Georgetown University and as senior fellow at the American Enterprise Institute (AEI). She also served on the President's Foreign Intelligence Advisory Board from 1985 to 1990 and the Defense Policy Review Board from 1985 to 1993, and chaired the Commission on Fail Safe and Risk Reduction of the nuclear command and control system in 1992.

In addition to her responsibilities at Georgetown and AEI, Dr. Kirkpatrick writes a syndicated column and speaks throughout the country, thus participating in the ongoing public dialogue on America's role in the world.

Her recent books include *The Withering Away of the Totalitarian State, Legitimacy and Force* (two volumes), *The Reagan Phenomenon, Dictatorships & Double Standards, Dismantling the Parties: Reflections on Party Reform and Party Decomposition, The New Presidential Elite, Political Woman,* and *Leader and Vanguard in Mass Society: A Study of Peronist Argentina.*

Dr. Kirkpatrick has received numerous awards and honors, primary among them the Medal of Freedom — the nation's highest civilian honor — in May 1985; two Department of Defense Distinguished Public Service Medals, the highest civilian honor in the Department of Defense; the French Prix Politique for political courage, and the Morgenthau Award of the American Council on Foreign Policy.

Dr. Kirkpatrick received her bachelor's degree from Barnard College, her master's and doctoral degrees from Columbia University, and studied at the Institut des sciences politiques de Paris.

Jeane J. Kirkpatrick

U.S. Ambassador to the United Nations
(1981-1985)

Jeane J. Kirkpatrick

[South China Sea Conference luncheon address delivered at the American Enterprise Institute, Washington, D.C., September 8, 1994.]

Recently China has made unprecedented claims to exclusive jurisdiction and has undertaken an unprecedented military build-up in the South China Sea. And we do not know why. We are not certain about the goals of China's leaders nor the means by which they will seek to attain those goals. We know neither what China will do, nor, more important, what it will not do in the South China Sea. Intent is always more important than military capacity.

Our concern is not prompted by China's military build-up in the South China Sea nor by its territorial claims. It is the conjunction of new claims, sharply increased air and sea power, and indications of an unwillingness to negotiate differences with the other half dozen countries who also have claims, that concerns us. China has made claims far beyond anything that could reasonably be conceived as lying within its territorial waters. It has declined to join in anything but bilateral negotiations. Does China intend to use force to establish control over the Spratly Islands' strategic sea lanes and its seabed minerals? Will it go to war to eliminate rival claimants to these valuable resources? The answers to the questions depend on the intentions and the operational code of the government of China.

Our concern about China's rapid military acquisitions and increasing military capacity is also mainly a function of uncertainty about its intentions. During the Cold War, Americans never were concerned about the United Kingdom's nuclear weapons and capacities. The fact that Britain had substantial nuclear forces or that France had large nuclear forces operating under an independent national control did not worry us because we thought we knew their intentions, and we believed those intentions to be benign. To the contrary, they were seen as strengthening our own.

Americans worried little about China's military build-up when the Soviet Union was deploying missiles and troops on its borders, invading Afghanistan and making assertive claims in the region. Then, it was reasonable to suppose China's intentions in modernizing and increasing its military forces were defensive. Now the same actions are more difficult to understand.

Now we do not know for certain how China intends to use its increasing capacities or why it is acquiring them. One authority wrote of China's build-up on Woody Island that it "signals an inclination to dominate the South China Sea by force rather than negotiate shared control with other claimants to the Spratlys." Does it? Is that what it signifies? Intent is the single most important element in assessing danger. And it is the element about which we know least.

We know the Spratly Islands have great strategic value — located as they are astride sea routes through which 25 percent of the world's shipping passes. We know that huge quantities of oil, gas and other valuable minerals may lie beneath the surface. We know, too, that China's 1989 geological studies enhanced their interest in these islands. The most recent studies — reported just this week — further heighten the expectation of huge quantities of natural resources. Of course, we also know China's industrial capacity is increasing rapidly, creating new needs for fuel, for gas and oil.

We also know China's rapid economic growth has been accompanied by an equally impressive increase in military power — though we don't know exactly why. China is engaged in the largest military build-up of any major power and at a time that the principal threat to it has all but disappeared. So what are China's intentions?

The strategic value of the scattered islands, the increased estimates of their economic value, their increased military power, and extended claim to the islands do not cast much light on whether the government of China will use force in the effort to establish exclusive control of these islands. This will depend on the intentions of China's leaders.

How its leaders use their power, what they think about it, will tell us more about their probable intentions in the South China Sea than will the current balance of forces. How can we know a government's intentions? How a government uses power in dealing with its own citizens provides important insights into how it is likely to behave in dealing with other governments.

There are compelling *strategic* reasons to be concerned with human rights records and practices of governments. Dissidents challenge a government's claim to exclusive power over the symbolic environment. A government's response to challenges from defenseless persons and groups inside the country offers insight into how it may deal with other challenges from other sources on other matters.

Restraint in the use of power in domestic affairs is relevant to restraint of use of power in dealing with other nations. Tolerance of opposition and respect for the rights of citizens is integrally related to respect for others in international affairs. The demand for a monopoly of power internally is dynamically related to the need for exclusive power outside.

In this violent century we have seen — again and again — that governments with the worst human rights records are also the most likely to commit aggression against neighbors, to start wars, and to impose their preferred positions on others by force.

Benito Mussolini's treatment of the Italian opposition foreshadowed his treatment of Ethiopia. Adolf Hitler's merciless destruction of Poland was foreshadowed, I believe, by his merciless treatment of Germany's Jews, gypsies and dissidents from Nazi rule. Joseph Stalin's proclivities concerning the use of force could be observed early in his treatment of Bolshevik and Menshevik rivals. He destroyed them. His treatment of the internal opposition told us all we needed to know to predict his later policies toward the Baltic states and the Poles.

The government of Iraq provides an interesting, current example of the relationship between aggression against the rights of citizens, and aggression beyond its borders. The total war waged by Iraq against Kuwait is of a piece with the total war being waged right now against Iraq's own Shi'ite population.

This link between human rights and peace is the same as the link between democracy and peace. It is widely understood today that democracies do not start aggressive wars, in part because people who must fight the wars are usually less enthusiastic about the risks entailed. But also because *democracy breeds habits of restraint in the use of power*, in dealing with differences, and tolerating opposition.

These linkages between a regime's human rights practices and its foreign policy are empirical and important. That is why we should — indeed, we must — take into account persistent human rights abuses by the Chinese government if we are to try to predict its actions with regard to the use of force in the South China Sea or elsewhere.

They are not the only factors that should be taken into account, but they must not be ignored. We dare not ignore the State Department's most recent human rights reports, for example, which tell us that China has indefinitely postponed its promised talks with the International Red Cross on providing access to prisons; that China has broken off discussions with the Voice of America on jamming broadcasts; that the government of China was continuing its arrests of religious leaders, and, as a matter of fact, increasing its arrests of religious, labor and democracy advocates; that China was continuing its mistreatment of prisoners including severe beatings and isolation, and that they continued their utilization of forced labor.

It is a fundamental, if common, mistake to treat a government's organization and use of power internally as irrelevant to strategic concerns. Some students of international affairs call "moralistic" a concern for a government's internal practices; regard it as unrelated to "strategic" matters. The fact that China is an authoritarian, one-party state which still denies its citizens basic civil and political liberties must be faced when we think about its intentions in the South China Sea. So must its lack of accountability.

In democracies, governments regularly submit their power to the requirements of law and the principle of consent.

Unwillingness of rulers to submit their actions to popular judgments, to share power or tolerate criticism, warns us that they may not be willing to share power or negotiate differences in external affairs. The uninhibited use of force against dissidents warns us that the government may use force to impose its will on external challengers as well.

The fate of Tibet cannot be assumed to be irrelevant to the fate of Hong Kong or Taiwan or any other distinctive community which becomes an object of China's ambition and absorption.

Of course, there are important differences between domestic victims of repression and independent states. Citizens of a country are more vulnerable to its government, more defenseless. What happens to them is less likely to become a public, much less an international issue. Disapproval by other governments and imposition of sanctions discourage repression even when the impulse to use force is strong.

In considering China's intentions we must also consider its ambitions and the global context in which China must operate today. The transition from a totalitarian to an authoritarian regime has already occurred in the People's Republic, and more changes are under way. Most of the important changes that have occurred so far have taken place as a consequence of decisions of Chinese leaders pursuing their own preferred goals — and not in response to external pressure. Crucial changes occurred as China's leaders came to understand that a powerful, modern nation (which they desire China to be) requires continuing economic and technological development, and this requires opening the country to contacts with persons who possess the skills, knowledge, and products of advanced technology. The same leaders not willing to limit their powers by law are willing to forego their control of the symbolic environment to achieve greater scientific and technological power. For the sake of growth and modernization, China's leaders sent tens of thousands of Chinese to study abroad and welcomed foreign specialists into China. This travel, trade, and scientific exchange required China to relax its controls on the symbolic environment.

Though the government still censors speech, press, radio and television, it lost control of the symbolic environment and opened itself to diverse foreign influences and temptations which created new incentives of the kind regularly found in "materialistic" Western societies. Openness bred success, and success reinforce openness.

The Chinese government opened itself to the world when the world was undergoing dramatic changes with special relevance to China. It opened itself to the world at the time when great political upheavals in the Soviet Union had begun to dismantle its socialist system and empire and political earthquakes were taking place in the West. China opened itself to the world at a time when Cold War alliances were disintegrating like an iceberg. It opened itself at a time when the New International Economic Order (NIEO) and the Non-Aligned Movement (NAM) — both of which had special importance for China — were themselves weakened almost beyond recognition.

China opened itself to the world when socialist countries in Europe and in Asia were turning to market strategies of development and choosing democratic options. Because of its enhanced contact with the world, China felt the full impact of this peaceable revolution and could not help noticing the declining credibility of Marxism and the increased importance of democracy as the legitimizing principle of organization of states.

China's leaders could not help noticing that many peoples acquired freedom in the process of modernizing, and observing this, determined to protect China against political reform. The "China model" for escaping the stagnation of totalitarianism emphasized market reforms, and rejected political liberalization. Or tried to. In fact, it could not avoid the impact of global developments. And like it or not, they have altered the possibilities open to China.

The collapse of the Soviet Union held special significance for the world's second most powerful Marxist-Leninist state. It left China's position both enhanced and diminished. It left China the only major Socialist power in the world, the only Socialist state with permanent member status in the United Nations, the victor in an intensely felt rivalry with the Soviet big brother, the victor in a contest for survival. It relieved China of the main threat to its security, and provided a new source of technology and weapons.

But on its way to becoming a world power, the foundation on which China stood shook beneath it. The dissolution of the Soviet Union and the Socialist world system meant the collapse of Marxism-Leninism as a competing paradigm for understanding the world and as a legitimizing myth, available to justify the socialist states' use and abuse of power.

Marxism's claim to have penetrated the laws of history is the ultimate basis of Marxist-Leninist states' and Communist parties' claim to legitimacy. Communist party leaders could claim infallibility and a monopoly of power because of their supposedly special relationship to historical processes and special understanding of them. But the dissolution of the Soviet Union and the dismantling of the Socialist world system suggested to almost everyone — including Fidel Castro — that Marxism-Leninism and the Soviet Union had been mistaken on some key points. They had been mistaken about the irreversibility of the revolution.

Fidel Castro recently said that his greatest mistake was to have overestimated the irreversibility of the "revolution" and the inevitability of its triumph. He was not the only one.

Meanwhile, the manifestly superior economic performance of capitalist societies undermined and finally eliminated the claims to superiority of the "Socialist model" of development. The Socialist economic model was simply discredited. With it went the associated ideologies and organizations: the NIEO and the Non-Aligned Movement.

The Chinese had seen themselves as the big brother of the Third World. China was the self-designated protector of the Non-Aligned Movement in various international bodies, the self-appointed representative of the less-developed nations, the spokesman for the "South" in North/South dialogues on redistribution of the world's wealth. The collapse of the Third World ideology demonstrated that it had been as dependent on Marxist-Leninist principles as the Soviet Union itself.

The collapse of Marxism-Leninism and the NIEO left the Chinese Communist Party exposed internationally and uncertain domestically — without a firm ideological base for its claim to exclusive power domestically. And as Rousseau emphasized, without a firm ideological base on which to rest its claim to legitimate power, no state can expect to long endure.

The collapse of this ideological, organizational foundation left the Chinese party and the Chinese state less certain of its expectations of a glorious future. The fact that its foundation was weakened at the time the world was moving to democracy, and the democratic idea was spreading like wild fire, further weakened the claim to legitimacy of Communist parties.

The dramatic, worldwide turn to democracy — in South America, Eastern Europe and Asia, and parts of Africa — coincided with the spread of a new democratic global ethos, according to which democracy and respect for human rights are the basis of legitimate government. The *only* basis of a legitimate government. The beliefs associated with a democratic political culture and the democratic ethos penetrated even the "Asian model" of the modernizing state and the Bangkok Declaration, which is often cited as proof of Asia's resistance to the spreading virus of democracy. While supposedly rejecting the notion of universal human rights, Asian leaders, nonetheless, affirmed: "While human rights are universal in nature, they must be considered in the context of a dynamic and evolving process of international norm-setting, bearing in mind the significance of national and regional particularities and various historical, cultural and religious backgrounds."

It is said that Asian leaders intended to make the point that "Western" rights may not be appropriate for non-Western societies. But even this group of representatives of the world's authoritarian states found it necessary to begin the definitive paragraph of the Declaration by affirming the universality of human rights.

These changes in the world occur, moreover, at a time that China is facing a generational change in leadership. Even closed societies cannot resist the replacement of one generation by the next. With his description of the deterioration of the ideal state, Plato provides a theory that explains how closed societies change. The Soviet Union provides a case study, illustrating how succession can bring to power a new generation of leaders with different goals and values, different perspectives and policies. Mikhail Gorbachev is an excellent example. It came as a shock to learn that the carefully planned, carefully recruited leaders expected to preserve the Soviet system might, nonetheless, bring to the top "new men" who transformed it.

An indispensable aspect of the dissolution of the Soviet Union was, I believe, the limited change in perspective and values which Mikhail Gorbachev and his colleagues, Alexander Yakolov and Eduard Shevardnadze, brought with them to the apex of power. All were somewhat more concerned about the Soviet Union's acceptability to the West, somewhat more concerned about the Soviet Union's lack of technical and economic progress, and somewhat less confident about the inevitability of the global triumph of their own system. All were less inclined to use force as a regular instrument of policy.

From small differences come large changes. I believe that the presence of a new generation near the top of the Chinese political system has already had its effects on China's government. Soon it will arrive at the top and rapidly transform the Chinese regime.

I think of President/General Charles deGaulle, who, when his critics complained that he would never relinquish power, would assure them that he, too, would surely die one day. And of course, he did. So will China's leaders. When that happens new leaders with new perspectives will take power at the apex of China's centralized system. The new leaders will be more affected by the new global democratic ethos. They will have seen more of the world. They will have been affected by the changing global political culture as an earlier generation was affected by Marx and Lenin. They will change China, which will, in any case, have already been changed by modernization's own dynamic.

Meanwhile it is necessary to remember that the government of China does not show reliable restraint in the use of power internally. But we should remember, too, that this Chinese regime is not reckless. It has not shown a taste for foreign adventures or unnecessary risks — so far. We cannot assume that China's leaders will act with reliable restraint abroad — except as the rest of the world provides clear incentives for it to do so. Clarity and firmness are needed from trading partners who have resources desired by this modernizing giant.

Waiting, never easy for Americans, may be all that is required. Whatever the Chinese government's intent in the South China Sea and the Taiwan Straits, today, the rest of us should clearly communicate our intentions of cooperation and our expectations that the South China Sea will be developed and the resources exploited on the basis of negotiation, agreement, and recognized international norms.

Hilda L. Solis

Senator Hilda L. Solis was elected to a newly reapportioned senatorial district in California in November of 1994. Upon her election, Solis made history by becoming the first Latina to ever serve in the California State Senate. Prior to being elected to the upper house of the Legislature, Solis served in the California Assembly from 1992 to 1994.

Solis serves as chair of the Senate Industrial Relations Committee, and is a member of the Finance, Investment, and International Trade; Health and Human Services; Judiciary; Natural Resources; and Public Employment and Retirement committees. She is also chair of the Subcommittee on the Underground Economy and the Work Force, and the Subcommittee on Asia Trade and Commerce.

During her tenure in the Legislature, Solis was named Freshman Legislator of the Year by the California School Boards Association and the California League of Conservation Voters. She has demonstrated a willingness to take on tough issues. Senator Solis focused her energies on improving the quality and access to California's educational system, addressed urban environmental issues, created better access to health care for underserved communities, and improved protection for victims of crime.

Senator Solis has authored legislation in the areas of domestic violence, environmental protection, education, and crime. She is a strong advocate of women's rights and a leading author of measures pertaining to women's health, restraining orders and spousal abuse.

Solis earned her bachelor of arts degree at California State Polytechnic University, Pomona, and her master's degree at the University of Southern California. She then served as editor-in-chief for the White House Office of Hispanic Affairs during the Carter administration in 1980. Solis also served as a management analyst for the U.S. Office of Management and Budget in Washington, D.C.

Upon returning to California, Solis became director of the California Student Opportunity and Access Program, serving several Los Angeles and Orange County school districts. She was elected to the Rio Hondo Community College Board of Trustees and served two terms from 1985 through 1992. In 1991, Solis was appointed to serve on the Los Angeles Country Insurance Commission.

Hilda L. Solis

State Senator
Democrat, California

Hilda L. Solis

[Speech delivered to the California State Senate, Sacramento, California, October 22, 1993.]

Rape is rape and it's that simple, right? Wrong!

One of the most tragic failures of our criminal justice system has been the perpetuation of numerous myths harmful to women made permanent by our own laws. Many people trivialize violence against women and children in the home because they still view a man's house as his castle. The marriage license has become more than just a document to constitute unity; it has become, in some cases, a license to kill.

My greatest reward as a legislator has been the opportunity to dismantle myths by changing outdated laws. This began with my Assembly Bill 187, which finally makes marital rape a felony offense. It's hard to imagine that we entered the 1990s without this law, but what a relief it was to achieve this protection.

Another hard-fought but successful effort was the establishment of a state data bank for all restraining orders issued in California. Now law enforcement personnel everywhere have restraining order information at their fingertips and the ability to respond appropriately.

Many of you in this room have been leaders fighting against domestic violence for over a decade. Your work has enabled legislation like mine to be enacted. District and city attorneys, sheriffs and police chiefs, and advocacy organizations like the California Alliance Against Domestic Violence have all been builders of a movement finally taking shape. You, probably more than anyone, realize what I have faced and learned as a result of pursuing these and other bills.

I quickly learned that curing domestic violence was not a popular topic to many interest groups and to many of my colleagues. The resistance I received during committee hearings was astounding, and some of the remarks made by witnesses and committee members were shocking. So many people still think a husband has unceasing rights to not only employ punishment as a means of controlling his wife, but to also sexually assault her.

I now understand why it has taken so long to pass legislation protecting the rights of women and their children, particularly in domestic violence cases. The barriers we face are not just the "good old boys' club;" surprisingly, they include other women and deeply held beliefs about the sanctity of the home. It has only been recently that public opinion has started to sway, recognizing violence as violence, whether it occurs in the home or not! Violence is no longer protected by household sanctity.

When statistics show that more than 4,000 people are killed annually by their partners and that intimate battery is the primary cause of injury to women, we know there is a problem. When studies demonstrate that domestic violence begins or becomes more acute upon pregnancy and that it is the No. 1 cause of birth defects, we know we're dealing with an epidemic. Even FBI data proves that 50 percent of all married women will be beaten in their lifetime.

Domestic violence is a poison not just within a household, but outside that home, affecting all of our lives. With the recognition of generational cycles of violence, we must continue to address this issue, even if it remains unpopular to many.

Sometimes we experience an overwhelming sense of frustration about the volume of work that remains. That is why it is important to look at where we've been.

Do you remember a time when domestic violence shelters were not available? The earliest shelters were born only about 20 years ago, most opening in the early 1980s. Before this time, there was no organized or institutional support for survivors of these crimes. Stalking laws and restraining orders are also a recent advent that have been helpful in the protection of victims.

There are numerous gains we can look to, feel proud about, catch our breath, and then say, "What's next?"

We know that restraining-order laws need to be improved upon and updated. We must do something to protect women, particularly those who are being stalked, from the fear and violence that often results in death. And we will have to investigate the more explosive issues regarding child custody and the effects of family violence on children.

The single most important thing we can do, however, is call for long-term planning so that we can continue to address these issues in an era where elected representatives face term limits. No longer can we turn to the same individuals, year in and year out, to shepherd fresh legislation and maintain the attention domestic violence deserves.

That is why I am calling for a statewide domestic violence conference next year in order to create a blueprint for California's future. We plan for our transportation needs, our educational structures, and our waste disposal sites. Why not plan to address the issue which threatens every effort to improve our society? Why not create a vision for our future rather than suspend our efforts with reactionary responses? Why not create a California where we're safe inside of our homes as well as outside of them?

Thank you.

Deborah J. Glick

Deborah Glick first ran for public office in 1990, when she became not only the assemblymember for lower Manhattan but also New York's first openly lesbian or gay state legislator. In 1992, Glick was re-elected with 98 percent of the vote, giving her the largest vote total in any New York Assembly district.

Glick's political activity began in college and her involvement in grassroots organizing continues today. She has focused on areas relating to civil rights, reproductive freedom, lesbian and gay rights, environmental improvement and preservation, and the arts. This involvement has shaped Glick's view of government and her role in it. Glick believes that to be effective in moving the world toward social justice for all people, government needs to be motivated by the activism of grassroots organizations and people. For that reason, Glick sees her job as one similar to a community organizer.

Assemblymember Glick is a lifelong resident of New York City. She received her B.A. from Queens College and her MBA from Fordham University. Having followed an unconventional career path — seven years as a production supervisor for Steinway Pianos, through a two-year stint as deputy director for the New York City Housing, Preservation and Development Agency — she has found that her experiences have kept her grounded with the needs of working people and the struggles of average individuals and families. The diverse skills she has assembled along with her managerial experience have taught her that "everyone must contribute their own valuable and diverse skills to help create a better society."

Assemblymember Glick chairs the Legislative Task Force on People with Disabilities and is vice chair of the Legislative Commission on Critical Transportation Choices. She is also a member of the following committees: Ways and Means, Environmental Conservation, Children and Families, Governmental Employees, Governmental Operations and Social Services.

Deborah J. Glick

State Assembly
Democrat, New York

Deborah J. Glick

[Speech delivered on the floor of the New York State Assembly, February 1, 1993.]

Note to the Editors from Assemblywoman Glick:

Thank you for contacting me about your project. I hope you will consider the inclusion of this speech. I had a prepared speech, which I intended to give on the floor of the New York State Assembly in support of the sexual orientation nondiscrimination bill. However, that plan was overturned when the Republican minority leader decided not to debate the bill.

By house rules, each member has the right to utilize two 15-minute periods to make their points for or against a measure being debated. However, if there is no debate, each member only has two minutes to explain their vote. For whatever strategic reasons, the minority decided to go right to a vote. Out the window went the prepared speech. For many people it was the first time that they heard the voice of an out lesbian or gay man speak on the issue of justice and equality for lesbians and gay men. It was also the first time that either house of the New York State Legislature had considered and passed an omnibus bill protecting lesbians and gay men from discrimination in the areas of housing, employment and public accommodations. What follows is the two-minute-plus extemporaneous speech, the text of which we have from the transcript of the proceedings.

It's particularly fitting that we pass this bill today, which is the first day of Black History Month. By passing this bill today, we act in the same spirit in the struggle for civil rights, the same spirit as Rosa Parks, Sojourner Truth and Thurgood Marshall.

It is, for me, a particularly emotional day. I have been out of the closet as a lesbian for 20 years. I have faced discrimination; I have faced discrimination as a Jew, as a woman, and as a lesbian. Each and every one of those circumstances were painful and they were wrong and there wasn't any difference between them.

It is important for everyone to understand the kind of struggle that we put young people through. I said that I came out 20 years ago, but long before that I knew I was a lesbian; but I also knew about prejudice, bigotry, discrimination and violence; and I tried, tried very hard, not to be gay because I understood hatred.

And I have heard people say that to be lesbian or gay is unnatural; it is only unnatural if you are not lesbian or gay. It is very natural for me.

I finally came to the decision and the realization that I had to be true to myself and so I took a step that some people have said is courageous, but it wasn't, it was what I had to do. It is who I am and I have been blessed by the fact that my family continues to love and support me.

We are not anti-family. We care deeply about our families and, because of that, many of us have tried not to come out because we don't want to subject them to hurt and to ridicule.

But it is incredibly important for this society to finally rid itself of the last vestiges of ignorance because it is ignorance that leads to prejudice and bigotry and it is bigotry that leads to violence that will destroy all of us, not just those who are the victims of that discrimination, but the entire society.

So I am very proud of you, my colleagues, because you have stood up today and said that it is time that New York State take the correct step toward ending one of those last painful condemnations of people for who they are.

It is not easy to live in a society that is filled with homophobia. There are places in this state where my rights, my rights as a member of this body, my rights are not protected; and there are many places in this country where that continues to be the case.

And there are people who think they know me because they know one thing about me, and all of their misconceptions come into play. All of you, whether you understand the feelings that I have, whether you voted yes or no, you are participating in a process that will result in all of us being freer.

Those of you who have voted yes, I thank you for your support. I thank you on behalf of all the citizens that you represent because I'm the only lesbian in my family, but I know that my sisters and my brothers-in-law and my nieces and nephews would thank you on my behalf; and I'm sure that goes many, many fold over for your constituents throughout this state.

And now we have a lot of work to do to see that it becomes the law of this state. We have taken the first step. Again, I thank you and I vote in the affirmative.

Rosalie E. Wahl

*J*ustice Rosalie E. Wahl completed her undergraduate studies in 1946 at the University of Kansas, and received her doctor of laws degree in 1967 from the William Mitchell College of Law.

She began her career as an assistant state public defender in Minnesota, a position she held for six years. She taught as a clinical professor at her alma mater, the William Mitchell College of Law, from 1973 until 1977. In 1977, Wahl became the first woman justice named to the Minnesota Supreme Court. Before her retirement in 1994, she had been joined by three additional women justices, which gave the first female majority to any high court in the United States.

Wahl was chair of the Minnesota Supreme Court's Racial Bias Task Force, the Task Force on Gender Fairness in the Courts and the Gender Fairness Implementation Committee. She was the court liaison with the Minnesota State Board of Law Examiners.

She served as chair of the American Bar Association's Section on Legal Education and Admissions to the Bar and chaired its Accreditation Committee. She also was a member of its Task Force on Law Schools and the Profession: Narrowing the Gap.

She holds memberships in legal organizations that include the American Law Institute, American Judicature Society, Minnesota State Bar Association, National Association of Women Judges, and Minnesota Women Lawyers.

Rosalie E. Wahl

Associate Justice, Minnesota Supreme Court
(1977-1994)

Rosalie E. Wahl

[Speech delivered to the Women Judges' Fund for Justice Luncheon at the National Association of Women Judges Annual Conference, Chicago, October 11, 1991.]

We have come together today in convention assembled — the National Association of Women Judges (NAWJ) and its Fund for Justice — after an exciting, tumultuous, disquieting year. We have come to take stock of our routs and our victories, to clear our vision, to renew our strength and our commitment to the work we have undertaken.

Some hard rain has fallen this year. We have seen the United States Supreme Court achieve the numbers and the will sufficient to dismantle and set aside — logically, rationally, dispassionately — protections for the disadvantaged and vulnerable, protections for us all, rights we have thought long established.

We have seen the ease with which the macho, military mind and a manipulated, manipulative media can turn a whole people overnight to that ultimate backlash against the values we espouse — WAR. Just as the status of women is rising, the power of the blade has been re-established.

We have seen billions of dollars poured into the destruction of human and natural resources in the Persian Gulf and the S & L bailout here at home without outrage or even complaint and yet — for all the taxes we pay — we have no money, or not enough, for state and local governments to pay their bills. We have no money, we are told, for programs and services essential to human life and health and dignity in our communities. No money for children, no money for education, no money for at-risk kids, no money for treatment programs, no money for job-training programs and jobs, no money for health care. We do have money, though, to keep more and more adults and juveniles in prison on longer and longer sentences.

It is not only downright discouraging — it is intolerable! Perhaps only its intolerability will move us and motivate us and save us. And yet we know — John Kenneth Galbraith has told us — that "people of privilege will risk their complete destruction rather than surrender any material part of their advantage."[1] And it is the surrender of privilege we are talking about.

Even as our nation grapples, as a drowning person, to hang onto its position of world dominance — if not world leadership — the world itself is standing on the threshold of new possibilities of cooperation and relationship. We, the people of this world, are standing at a critical juncture of social evolution.

Riane Eisler, in her significant and challenging book, *The Chalice and the Blade*, proposes that *underlying the great surface diversity of human culture are two basic models of society. The first,* [which she calls] *the dominator model, is what is popularly termed either patriarchy or matriarchy — the ranking of one half of humanity over the other. The second, in which social relations are primarily based on the principle of linking rather than ranking, may best be described as the partnership model. In this model — beginning with the most fundamental difference in our species, between male and female — diversity is not equated with either inferiority or superiority.*[2]

It may be, as Eisler concludes, that the dominator model has reached its logical limits at our level of technological development. And it also may be that whether we move into "the new era of a partnership world through new ways of structuring politics, economics, science, and spirituality"[3] depends on the determination, the insistence and the leadership of the women of the world, including the women judges of the world.

Käthe Kollwitz has a wonderfully powerful lithograph called *Tower of Mothers* in which a group of absolutely fierce, unmovable women are protecting a group of children within the circle of their bodies.[4] When I look at that picture, I think of women judges. I think of you. I think of Judge Harriet Lansing's opinion for a majority in a divided court of appeals (five male judges dissenting) that upheld the male trial judge's order to increase the spousal maintenance and said it should be higher than he had ordered because he had failed to take into account hundreds of dollars per month in medical expenses.[5] I think of Judge Mary Winter finishing a term in family court, saying, "I don't want kids to live in impoverished households. I am perceived as pro-women, but I see it as pro-kids."[6]

We are making progress, we are doing a lot of the right things. And the NAWJ and the Women Judges' Fund for Justice play a significant role in the doing of those "right things" in our state court systems. The projects developed by the Fund for Justice are unique — and uniquely necessary. As Marilyn Nejelski, executive director of the Women Judges' Fund for Justice, has said: "Most of our issues — gender bias, bioethics, family violence — were created and shaped by us. It wouldn't occur to any other national judicial education provider to have a program on spousal support as we did as part of a[n] SJI grant last year."[7] Minnesota was one of three pilot states on that project. At the judicial conference where the program was presented, as our judges were fighting to get into the room where the program was being held at our annual judges' meeting (a room that held only 80), I overheard one judge saying to another (both male, of course), "Thank goodness they aren't having any of those 'gender fairness' programs this year."

The Woman Judges' Fund for Justice has also presented judicial selection seminars for women interested in pursuing appointments to state courts. I don't think anyone from Minnesota attended but we seem to be doing all right. Maybe you saw David Margolick's article in the *New York Times*, February 22, 1991: *Women's Milestone: Majority on Minnesota Court*. That article literally went around the world — *The Chicago Tribune, The Los Angeles Daily Journal, The London Times, The International Herald Tribune*,[8] and even *The Caney (Kansas) Chronicle*,[9] which claimed me, a country-girl outsider in my high school days, as a Caney native. "Ah, fame could not outrun me on the longest day!"[10]

Here are the opening paragraphs of that story:

> *Everyone knows that women are entering the legal profession in record numbers. But no powerful legal institution — no law school faculty, no large corporate law firm, no appellate court — has ever been dominated by women. Until now.*
>
> *Last month, in the waning moments of his tenure, Gov. Rudy Perpich of Minnesota named a fourth woman, Sandra Gardebring, to that state's Supreme Court. When she was sworn in on Jan. 4, it marked the first time that women had achieved the most critical of critical masses on a court of last resort: a majority.*
>
> *It is no longer news when a woman is named to a state supreme court. Currently, at least one sits on 27 of them. But for the most part, one is where the count has remained, just as it has on the United States Supreme Court. Only one state, Oklahoma, has two women on its highest court, and none have three.*
>
> *But the first woman named to the Minnesota Court, Rosalie E. Wahl, named by Governor Perpich in 1977, turned out to be more prelude than token. A second woman, M. Jeanne Coyne, was appointed by Gov. Albert Quie in 1982. Governor Perpich named the third, Esther M. Tomljanovich, in August 1990 and Judge Gardebring on his last work day in office.*
>
> *No one is predicting that the new female majority on the seven-member Minnesota court will instantly produce changes in its jurisprudence, though some lawyers anticipate heightened sensitivity to cases involving domestic abuse, child custody, spousal support, sexual harassment, employment discrimination and other issues of traditional concern to women.*[11]

If I were to choose a text from that story to guide us all, it would be this: "More prelude than token." The story, however, is wrong in two regards: First, we don't want to make instant changes in our jurisprudence — only significant ones — and those in a principled way in the proper time and case. And, second, we don't dominate the court, we don't want to. We only want our values and the law to relate in a way that will do justice — to the law and to the people that law serves.

Nothing that NAWJ and the Fund for Justice have done is of more significance than their development of the Gender Bias Task Force Model and their continuing support of the task force work and implementation efforts in all our states. Now we must commit our energies and hearts, every woman judge wherever we are, to help establish and work with task forces on racial bias of equal depth and scope. We must be agents of social change in the courts for race as well as gender.

Minnesota is now among the first half dozen or so states to explore the extent to which racial bias exists in our state court system. What, you may ask, is the urgency of such a study? And what does a study of racial bias in the courts mean for those of us who are white? Aren't we just intending to find out if "they" — people of color, that is, — are disadvantaged in the system and, if they are, to educate judges to be more sensitive?

Dr. John Taborn, a social scientist/psychologist/African-American studies professor, and member of our task force, has helped us on the task force put into context the urgency of a race bias study in our multicultural society. Dr. Taborn reduced the world and its population to a group of 100 persons. Of that 100 persons, Dr. Taborn said, 57 are Asians, 21 European, 14 North/South Americans, eight Africans. Of that 100 persons: 70 are non-white, 30 white;

70 are non-Christian, 30 Christian; six Americans hold 50 percent of the wealth; 80 live in substandard housing; 50 are malnourished, 50 are not hungry; 70 are illiterate, 30 are literate; one has a university education.

Dr. Taborn also informed us that, according to figures obtained from UNICEF, one in three persons entering the work force will soon be a person of color. This is the world in which we live. And if, as Woodrow Wilson said, "A constitutional government is as good as its courts," we had better look to the way people of color perceive they are treated by our courts, and how they are treated, to preserve the integrity of our system of justice, and, thus, of constitutional government.

As to what racial bias and a study of racial bias mean for those of us who are white, and we are the majority at this time in this country, I ask you to consider with me what privileges each of us has because of the color of our skin and how we can be accountable for those privileges.

Peggy McIntosh, scholar and associate director of the Wellesley College Center for Research on Women, through her work with male privilege, has identified and described white privilege.[12] Describing white privilege, she says, makes one newly accountable. "Thinking through unacknowledged male privilege as a phenomenon, [she] realized that since hierarchies in our society are interlocking, there was most likely a phenomena of white privilege which was similarly denied and protected." She realized that, as white persons, we have "been taught about racism as something which puts others at a disadvantage, but [have] been taught not to see one of its corollary aspects, white privilege, which puts us at an advantage." As whites we "are carefully taught not to recognize white privilege." Peggy McIntosh has "come to see white privilege as an invisible package of unearned assets which I can count on cashing in each day but about which I was 'meant' to remain oblivious." White privilege, she says, "is like an invisible weightless knapsack of special provisions, maps, passports, codebooks, visas, clothes, tools and blank checks."

Would each person here who is white look into your knapsack? Take a minute or two to identify some of the daily effects of white privilege in your life — things you can expect that your African-American, Asian-American, Hispanic and American Indian friends and co-workers, for the most part, cannot expect.

We who are white can, for the most part, Peggy McIntosh suggests:

1. Arrange to be in the company of people of our race most of the time.
2. If we should need to move, we can be pretty sure of renting or purchasing housing in an area which we can afford and in which we would want to live.
3. We can be pretty sure that our neighbors in such a location will be neutral or pleasant to us.
4. We can go shopping alone most of the time, pretty well assured that we will not be followed or harassed.

5. We can turn on the television or open to the front page of the paper and see people of our race widely represented.
6. We can be sure that our children will be given curricular materials that testify to the existence of their race. We can send our children to school knowing they will be judged according to themselves, not their color.
7. Whether we use checks, credit cards, or cash, we can count on our skin color not to work against the appearance of financial reliability.
8. We can arrange to protect our children most of the time from people who might not like them.
9. We can swear, or dress in second-hand clothes, or not answer letters, without having people attribute these choices to the bad morals, the poverty, or the illiteracy of our race.
10. We can do well in a challenging situation without being called a credit to our race.
11. We are never asked to speak for all the people of our racial group.
12. We can be pretty sure that if we ask to talk to "the person in charge," we will be facing a person of our race.
13. If a traffic cop pulls us over or if the IRS audits our tax return, we can be sure we haven't been singled out because of our race.
14. We can easily buy posters, postcards, picture books, greeting cards, dolls, toys, and children's magazines featuring people of our race.
15. We can go home from most meetings of organizations we belong to feeling somewhat tied in, rather than isolated, out-of-place, outnumbered, unheard, held at a distance, or feared.
16. We can take a job with an affirmative action employer without having co-workers on the job suspect that we got it because of race.
17. We can be sure that if we need legal or medical help, our race will not work against us.
18. We can choose blemish cover or bandages in "flesh" color and have them more or less match our skin.[13]

And, I suggest, we can — as lawyers — appear in court and expect to be recognized as the lawyer, not the defendant.

Only as those of us who are white continue to work to identify and acknowledge how unearned race advantage and conferred dominance actually affect our daily lives — only then is systemic change possible. And all of us together need to listen to and to learn from the lives and experiences of those who have not had an invisible knapsack of unearned privilege.

We need to listen to the words of Peggy Davis, African-American New York University law professor and member of the New York State Judicial Commission on Minorities, in her devastating article, *Law as Microaggression*.[14] Microaggressions are "subtle, stunning, often automatic, and non-verbal exchanges which are 'put downs' of blacks by offenders.

Psychiatrists who have studied black populations view them as 'incessant and cumulative' assaults on black esteem"[15] which require preoccupying management.

Peggy Davis also discusses the experience of three black jurors who had their views disregarded by white jurors:

> *These jurors know from experiences inside and outside the courthouse that racial stereotypes and assumptions of white superiority permeate society to create cognitive drifts in the direction of findings of black culpability and white victimization, black incompetence and white competence, black immorality and white virtue, black indolence and white industriousness, black lasciviousness and white chastity, blacks careless and in need of control and whites in control and controlling, blacks as social problems and whites as valued citizens. These cognitive drifts render fragile a wide variety of factual claims: the defense of a black parent charged with child neglect; the claim that the potential and quality of a black life has been impaired by a white person's negligence; the defense of a black accused of malpractice; the credibility of a black witness; the worth of the opinion of a black expert; the merits of a black tenant's request for a stay of eviction; a black woman's claim of rape. To a people under the influence of microaggression, the expectation of unbiased judicial fact-finding is naive.*[16]

Davis concludes her article with these words:

> *So long as legal decision-making excludes black voices, and hierarchial judgments predicated upon race are allowed insidiously to infect decisions of fact and formulations of law, minorities will perceive, with cause, that courts are fully capable — and regularly guilty — of bias. Minority communities will therefore continue to struggle with a mixed message of law: announced as the legitimate assertion of collective authority, but perceived as microaggression.*[17]

We need to listen, also, to the words of Robert Hickman as I heard them night before last at a public hearing of our Race Bias Task Force in St. Paul. Mr. Hickman, a sixth-generation Minnesotan, a teacher who has worked with at-risk youth for 30 years in the St. Paul public schools, told the task force members that he was afraid of the justice system; that many people had stayed away from the hearing because of fear. "Fear of the criminal justice system," he said, "is just as bad as bias." "What should be done?" we asked. "People overcome fear when they feel they are involved. Say — 'Come sit with us and help us work on this problem that is tearing us apart.'"[18]

Here I will stop but in closing I want to say this:

When we come to lay down — or to lift up — our work and our lives, may it be said of each of us, as it was said on this marble slab in the Old Meeting House Burying Ground in Jaffrey, New Hampshire:

SARAH AVERILL
DIED
OCT. 16, 1881
89 YRS, 5 MO, 5 DAYS
"SHE DONE ALL SHE COULD."

1. Galbraith, John Kenneth, *The Risks of Privilege*, Mpls. Star Trib., Jan. 27, 1983.
2. R. Eisler, *The Chalice and the Blade* at xvii (1988).
3. *Id.* at xxiii.
4. See M.C. Klein & H.A. Klein, *Käthe Kollwitz: Life in Art* 141 (1975).
5. Eichenholz v. Eichenholz, 407 N.W.2d 699 (Minn. Ct, App. 1987).
6. Peterson, *Women judges shifting balance in sex-based cases*, Mpls. Star Trib., Dec. 23, 1990.
7. Letter from Marilyn Nejelski to Justice Rosalie Wahl (Sept. 20, 1991).
8. *See. e.g.*, Margolick, *A New Majority: Minnesota sets a precedent on its state supreme court*, Chicago Trib., Mar. 31, 1991; Margolick, *A Critical Breakthrough*, L.A. Daily J., Feb. 28, 1991.
9. *Caney native makes history on woman-dominated state court*, Caney Chron., Apr. 17, 1991, at 1.
10. Dickinson, Emily.
11. Margolick, *Women's Milestone: Majority on Minnesota Court*, N.Y. Times, Feb. 22, 1991.
12. McIntosh, *White Privilege: Unpacking the Invisible Knapsack*, Peace and Freedom, July/Aug. 1989, at 10.
13. *Id.* at 10-11.
14. Davis, *Law as Microaggression*, 98 Yale L.J. 1559 (1989).
15. *Id.* at 1565 [quoting J. Dovidio & S. Gaertner, Prejudice, Discrimination, and Racism 84 (1986)].
16. *Id.* at 1571.
17. *Id.* at 1577.
18. Public Hearing, Minnesota Supreme Court Task Force on Racial Bias in the Courts, St. Paul Technical College, St. Paul, Minn., Oct. 9, 1991.

Cheryl A. Lau

Cheryl A. Lau became general counsel to the U.S. House of Representatives on January 4, 1995. Her appointment was made by the speaker of the House after she went through the application and interview process. As general counsel, Lau reports to the speaker and the Bipartisan Legal Advisory Group, which includes the majority and minority leadership and whips in the House of Representatives. Lau and her staff provide nonpartisan legal representation to all the members of Congress and to the institution itself.

Lau served as the vice chair of the 1992 Republican National Platform Committee and as secretary of the 1992 Republican National Convention. In addition, Lau is an active co-chair of the Republican "National Policy Forum" and is examining ways to reduce the size and scope of government.

Prior to her appointment as general counsel, Lau was elected in 1990 as the secretary of state of Nevada. In 1991, she secured legislative approval for sweeping changes in Nevada's corporate law, making Nevada more hospitable to corporate entities. In 1993, Lau was active in championing election reform in the state Legislature. Her work earned her Common Cause's "Ethics in Government" award, as well as other commendations.

As a member and past chair of the Nevada Women's Commission, Lau has examined critical issues such as domestic violence, the "glass ceiling," and role modeling for young women at risk. She fought to preserve the beauty of Lake Tahoe as a member of the Tahoe Regional Planning Agency. Lau was active in other community foundations as well.

Before entering politics, Lau worked as a deputy attorney general in Nevada from 1987 to 1990. She was also a legal researcher assigned to the Nevada Department of Transportation from 1981 to 1982.

Lau holds a J.D. from the University of San Francisco, a doctorate in musicology from the University of Oregon, a master's degree in music and psychology from Smith College and a bachelor's degree in music/education from Indiana University.

Cheryl A. Lau

General Counsel
U.S. House of Representatives

Cheryl A. Lau

[Excerpt from an address delivered at Rotary International District 761 in Vienna, Virginia, May 1995.]

Americans used to have a passionate distaste for "four-letter words." We would wash our kids' mouths out with soap for saying them. Now we seem to be surrounded by four-letter words on television and in the movies. Four-letter words are spray-painted on walls and freeway interchanges. Yet, one of the most important four-letter words is never used by graffiti artists and rarely used in daily conversation. That word is VOTE.

But say it we must, for the right to vote lies at the heart of democratic government. Voting is the engine which drives the vehicles of change and public service, and voter participation fuels that engine.

The ancient Greeks knew this, and they made voting as simple as possible. They voted with white rocks for "yes" and black rocks for "no." What was a gray rock for? "None of the above," of course!

But in the modern world, much can be said about voter participation and the decline of American democracy.

Each night on the news, we are bombarded with "proof positive" that the American voter is disenchanted, apathetic, angry, uncaring, uninformed, and a panoply of other gloomy terms. On a national level, however, little concerted effort was given to correcting this growing problem.

Until now.

For perhaps the first time in our history, national organizations came together under one umbrella as shelter from the storm that beset American democracy. The National Commission for the Renewal of American Democracy — known as Project Democracy — is a unique approach. This nonprofit project includes representation from literally all of the major players in the field of elections and voter outreach. Credibility isn't a problem for this group. Project Democracy is armed with research supplied by the Kettering Foundation. One recent Kettering report, Citizens and Politics, has served as our cornerstone. But more data, and especially data on the relationship between issues and participation, is our goal.

At issue today is how do we reconnect citizens and politics? Project Democracy has undertaken the task of discovering the path. Our purpose is to create change and to find concrete ways to act on this challenge.

We started by stimulating nationwide discussion on how to rebuild the connection between citizens and politics, identify promising initiatives from across America that helped to do this, and by setting forth an action agenda to disseminate these reports and make these initiatives a reality in communities throughout the 50 states.

The results are tangible, workable plans that could actually make a difference in stemming the tide of declining voter turnout. I think that's in keeping with what Americans deserve and even demand from government: answers, not more questions.

Victor Hugo once said that initiative is doing the right thing without being told. Project Democracy represents real initiative — we went and found the answers. We asked, before we were told, and listened once the telling had begun.

I am still a newcomer to public life. But I have learned what many others have learned over the years: there is a rising tide in this country, and it is a tide which demands action — not reaction.

Many people today still believe that government is not listening. That is why fewer Americans vote, and we must find ways to reverse that trend.

For therein lies the root of the problem we face: not only are voter turnouts low, they continue to decline in real terms.

In my state of Nevada, for example, voter turnout declined from 58 percent in 1960 to less than 45 percent in 1988. If 13 truly is an unlucky number, we were missing an unlucky 13 percent of our electorate! And we wanted them back. Like so many of my secretary of state colleagues, I made voter registration and participation the central tenets of my administration. And I can't tell you how inspiring Project Democracy has been for me.

Declining voter turnout percentages — many quite similar to those in Nevada — can be found in virtually every state, county and other political jurisdiction in the nation. This threat cuts across all ages and income groups. No election official can ignore the disturbing trends we see on a day-to-day basis.

Obviously, none of you can ignore these trends either. You care enough to listen to me.

Your support is vital to American democracy itself. Voter participation must be restored every election year — not at some distant future point. We can reverse the disturbing trends that confront our system, but we can only do so with a unified front. You may recall these words from Plato: "The punishment suffered by the wise who refuse to take part in government is to live under the government of bad men."

You may be called to the front lines in defense of that little four-letter word, VOTE. And know that I will be there with you.

Thank you.

Index of Issues   Page

Affirmative Action — Corrine Brown	69
Assault Weapons Ban — Dianne Feinstein	35
Child Neglect/Youth Policies — Tipper Gore	17
Court System Gender Bias — Rosalie E. Wahl	127
Domestic Violence — Hilda L. Solis	117
Economy/Global — Kay Bailey Hutchison	41
Education/Business/Community Partnerships — Madeleine May Kunin	97
Foreign Policy	
Arms Trade — Cynthia McKinney	77
China/Human Rights/Military Build-up in South China Sea — Jeane J. Kirkpatrick	107
Global Military Alliances — Kay Bailey Hutchison	41
Texas/Mexico Trade — Ann Richards	53
United States/Africa Relations — Nancy Landon Kassebaum	23
Girls' State/Girls' Responsibility For Their Future — Ann Richards	53
Health Care/Women's Health Issues — Patricia Schroeder	61
Human Rights/Abuses — Hillary Rodham Clinton	3
National Defense/Military Spending — Tillie K. Fowler	73
Presidency of the United States	
Running for Office — Lynn Martin	91
Obstacles for Women — Patricia Schroeder	61
Public Policy/Women's Advantages as Leaders — Elizabeth Dole	83
Racial Bias in Legal System — Rosalie E. Wahl	125
Sexual Orientation/Anti-Discrimination Law — Deborah J. Glick	121
United Nations	
Reform — Nancy Landon Kassebaum	28
Role — Hillary Rodham Clinton	9
Roosevelt, Eleanor — Hillary Rodham Clinton	9
Urban Strategy — Christine Todd Whitman	49
Voters/Project Democracy — Cheryl A. Lau	137
Voting Rights Act — Corrine Brown	69

DORIS EARNSHAW studied political science at Middlebury College, Vermont, and attended the Middlebury Summer Schools of French and Russian. She received her Ph.D. in comparative literature at the University of California, Berkeley. While a graduate student she organized the research and translation of women poets from many languages. She started Alta Vista Press on retirement from the faculty of the University of California. *American Women Speak* is the second in a series of three "Women Speak" books published by Alta Vista Press: *California Women Speak* (1994) and *International Women Speak* (scheduled for release in 1996).

MARÍA ELENA RAYMOND has been a print and television journalist for 20 years. During her 15 years in television she was elected to four years as a governor on the board of the San Francisco chapter of the National Academy of Television Arts and Sciences. She served a two-year term as a trustee of the national board. Now retired, she is a writing consultant for television news and public relations firms, and a guest host for on-line conferences on Compuserve when the focus is on women writers. For the past year she has worked as co-editor with Dr. Earnshaw on *American Women Speak*. She is also preparing a major bibliography of works by and about African-Americans in the post-Civil War era.

Type Styles Used: Dutch 801 Roman
Commercial Script-wp
Fonts found in WordPerfect 6.0
Paper Used: James River 601b White Recycled Offset

 PRINTED ON RECYCLED PAPER